Cambridge

Elements in Economics
edited by
Bruno S. Sergi
Harvard University

PUBLIC–PRIVATE DIALOGS TO SPUR EXPORT-LED GROWTH

The Case of Productivity Taskforces in Namibia

Andrés Fortunato
The Growth Lab at Harvard Kennedy School

Miguel Angel Santos
Escuela de Gobierno y Transformacion Publica, Tecnologico de Monterrey

Shaftesbury Road, Cambridge CB2 8EA, United Kingdom

One Liberty Plaza, 20th Floor, New York, NY 10006, USA

477 Williamstown Road, Port Melbourne, VIC 3207, Australia

314–321, 3rd Floor, Plot 3, Splendor Forum, Jasola District Centre, New Delhi – 110025, India

103 Penang Road, #05–06/07, Visioncrest Commercial, Singapore 238467

Cambridge University Press is part of Cambridge University Press & Assessment, a department of the University of Cambridge.

We share the University's mission to contribute to society through the pursuit of education, learning and research at the highest international levels of excellence.

www.cambridge.org
Information on this title: www.cambridge.org/9781009565325

DOI: 10.1017/9781009396141

© Andrés Fortunato and Miguel Angel Santos 2025

This publication is in copyright. Subject to statutory exception and to the provisions of relevant collective licensing agreements, with the exception of the Creative Commons version the link for which is provided below, no reproduction of any part may take place without the written permission of Cambridge University Press & Assessment.

An online version of this work is published at doi.org/10.1017/9781009396141 under a Creative Commons Open Access license CC-BY-NC-ND 4.0 which permits re-use, distribution and reproduction in any medium for non-commercial purposes providing appropriate credit to the original work is given. You may not distribute derivative works without permission. To view a copy of this license, visit https://creativecommons.org/licenses/by-nc-nd/4.0

When citing this work, please include a reference to the DOI 10.1017/9781009396141

First published 2025

A catalogue record for this publication is available from the British Library

ISBN 978-1-009-56532-5 Hardback
ISBN 978-1-009-39613-4 Paperback
ISSN 2631-8598 (online)
ISSN 2631-858X (print)

Cambridge University Press & Assessment has no responsibility for the persistence or accuracy of URLs for external or third-party internet websites referred to in this publication and does not guarantee that any content on such websites is, or will remain, accurate or appropriate.

Public–Private Dialogs to Spur Export-led Growth

The Case of Productivity Taskforces in Namibia

Elements in Economics of Emerging Markets

DOI: 10.1017/9781009396141
First published online: February 2025

Andrés Fortunato
The Growth Lab at Harvard Kennedy School

Miguel Angel Santos
Escuela de Gobierno y Transformacion Publica, Tecnologico de Monterrey

Author for correspondence: Andrés Fortunato, andres_fortunato@hks.harvard.edu

Abstract: This Element examines the implementation of Namibia's first Productivity Task Force (PTF) focused on the high-value fruit sector from 2021 to 2024. Productivity task forces, modeled after Peru's Mesas Ejecutivas, facilitate public–private dialogues to resolve sector-specific productivity issues. The Namibian Investment Promotion and Development Board, the Ministry of Agriculture, Water and Land Reform, and the Ministry of Finance led the Namibian task force. The element highlights critical stages, including the task force's management and organization, political authorization, and the identification and resolution of productivity problems. While some challenges remain unsolved, the PTF has laid the groundwork for long-term improvements in government capacity, better public–public coordination, public–private collaboration, and a more business-friendly environment. The Element offers valuable insights for implementing similar public–private initiatives in other developing countries. This title is also available as Open Access on Cambridge Core.

This Element also has a video abstract: Cambridge.org/EEM_Fortunato

Keywords: industrial policy, public–private dialogs, development economics, Productivity Task Forces, Namibia

© Andrés Fortunato and Miguel Angel Santos 2025

ISBNs: 9781009565325 (HB), 9781009396134 (PB), 9781009396141 (OC)
ISSNs: 2631-8598 (online), 2631-858X (print)

Contents

1 Introduction: Productivity Task Forces as Public–Private Dialog (PPD) — 1

2 The Context of Productivity Task Forces in Namibia — 5

3 Setting Up the Task Force — 11

4 Running the Task Force: Identifying Problems and Advancing Solutions — 28

5 In Hindsight: Assessing the Impact of the High-Value Fruits PTF — 44

6 A Roadmap for Productivity Task Forces: Reflections from Namibia — 52

7 Conclusions — 62

References — 65

List of Abbreviations — 70

1 Introduction: Productivity Task Forces as Public–Private Dialog (PPD)

The quest for economic growth through productivity gains is a fundamental challenge for small developing economies like Namibia. One effective strategy to address this challenge is the implementation of robust public–private dialogs (PPDs) at the sector level. These dialogs serve as platforms where government entities and representatives from the private sector work together to identify and solve sector-specific issues, thereby enhancing productivity or competitiveness and enabling the sector to tap into international markets' demand. This case study documents the experience of a PPD at the sector level carried in Namibia between 2021 and 2023 – labeled as Productivity Task Force (PTF) – focused on addressing coordination failures and boosting competitiveness in the high-value fruits sector. To the extent of our knowledge, this is the first effort to document a PPD at the sector level in Africa. By providing a detailed account of the experience and the sequence of processes it entails – defining the entity that will host and facilitate the dialogs, setting up the task force, selecting the sector, interviewing and screening the private sector representatives that will participate, identifying key issues and potential solutions, and mobilizing the public and private sectors into their implementation; evaluating and adapting the strategy – we hope to contribute to the growing literature on industrial policy in general and PPDs in particular. Our goal is to provide valuable lessons to policy practitioners.

In the context of fast technological changes and globalization, economic sectors must comply with international standards – environmental, sanitary, labor, and quality – to successfully insert their products into global markets. Productivity improvements require overcoming coordination failures at various levels: between the public and private sectors, within the private sector itself, and among different public sector entities. Traditional industrial policies, often broad and transversal, fail to address these coordination dilemmas at the sector level. Instead, modern industrial policy must be data-driven and sector-specific, providing essential public goods that improve competitiveness and leveling the playing field.

Public–private dialogs can facilitate strategic collaboration and play a pivotal role in modern industrial policy. Such collaboration involves shared diagnosis, problem identification, learning, experimenting with different solutions, monitoring results, and continuous adaptation. This iterative process helps build a shared vision of sectoral competitiveness and effectively addresses the most pressing productivity constraints.

An early example of successful PPDs at the sector level occurred at Malaysia's Performance Management and Delivery Unit (PEMANDU). Established in 2009 under the administration of Prime Minister Najib Razak, PEMANDU aimed to drive Malaysia's economic transformation program through strategic public–private collaboration established for a group of selected sectors (palm oil, rice, tourism, and electronics) and production factors (public transportation, national police, education, and environmental remediation). PEMANDU's approach involved setting clear goals, regular monitoring, and a focus on accountability, significantly improving the implementation of national policies and initiatives within the selected economic activities. The unit facilitated dialogs between various government agencies and private sector stakeholders to identify and address bottlenecks, enhance productivity, and ensure the timely delivery of projects. The success of PEMANDU in achieving its targets underscores the effectiveness of a structured, performance-driven approach to PPDs (Sabel & Jordan, 2015).

One of the most prominent examples of successful PPDs at the sector level are the *Mesas Ejecutivas* (ME) in Peru. Initiated in 2014 by the Ministry of Production under the leadership of Piero Ghezzi, these sector-specific working groups brought together key stakeholders from the public and private sectors to address issues such as red tape, market access, infrastructure problems, and innovation incentives. MEs were structured around strategic collaboration in eight selected sectors (forestry, aquaculture, creative industries, textiles, food services, agriculture exports, logistics, and entrepreneurship), bringing together relevant public and private stakeholders with firsthand knowledge of the day-to-day challenges and opportunities. This inclusive approach ensured that dialogs were grounded in practical realities and that the proposed solutions were feasible and impactful. The ME model emphasized the importance of regular, periodic meetings where stakeholders could engage in continuous dialog, identify barriers to higher productivity, define solutions, follow up through implementation, monitor progress, and adapt strategies as needed. This iterative process was crucial in building trust and fostering a shared vision for sectoral competitiveness. Ghezzi (2017, 2019) documented the successes and challenges of the Peruvian MEs, providing valuable insights for other countries seeking to implement similar initiatives. The Peruvian model demonstrated that effective PPDs require clear strategic leadership with significant authority within the government and a dedicated team to organize, run, and coordinate the dialogs, ensuring they are action-oriented. The MEs did not seek to replace existing structures but complemented them by addressing issues not typically tackled or prioritized by traditional government agencies. This approach improved private sector competitiveness and enhanced the efficiency of existing public sector structures.

Following Peru's example, Argentina implemented sectoral mesas between 2016 and 2019. The Argentine experience offers additional lessons on public–private dialogs. Initially, these mesas were more research-oriented and less action-focused, leading to significant delays and limited impact. These working groups did not have the same level of political support as the Peruvian MEs and lacked regular working schedules. Instead, the Argentine mesas were launched as a kind of master plan focused on problems and solutions that had been predefined and did not require follow-up. All these factors led to the decision to discontinue the initiative in 2017. In 2018, they were relaunched by a different group of government officials, adopting a more structured approach similar to the Peruvian model, resulting in greater effectiveness and impact. Obaya and Stein (2021) highlight the importance of political support, structured dialogs, and continuous engagement in achieving successful outcomes.

The Peruvian and Argentina cases are two of the most recent, structured, and better documented but by no means are the only PPDs at the sector level in Latin America. There is a significant array of efforts that involve some form of PPDs with different goals, methodologies, and results, all with relevant lessons for policy practitioners. Crespi et al. (2014) provide an overview of several cases along with a conceptual framework for industrial policy design, and Fernandez-Arias et al. (2016) document the diverse experience of Costa Rica, Chile, and Uruguay with these policy instruments. Mexico also undertook some form of PPDs, not at the sector level, but rather to explore the economic potential of certain regions at the subnational level (Devlin & Pietrobelli, 2016). Then there is the case of the *Consejo Privado de la Competitividad* (Private Competitiveness Council) and the *Comisiones Regionales de Competitividad* (Regional Competitiveness Commissions) in Colombia (Gómez Restrepo & Mitchell, 2016). More recently, there were efforts organized in Argentina to address the internationalization agenda of productive development policies (Hallak & López, 2022), the coordination problems within agriculture and food systems (González et al., 2022), and the case of PPDs in the sweet cherries sector (Jaurequiberry & Tappata, 2022). Other documented cases of PPDs include Egypt, Lebanon, Malta, Turkey, and Spain (World Bank, 2011).

Aside from the experiences mentioned earlier, other relevant pioneering examples include the Korean Export Council of the 1960s (Schneider, 2015) and the Japan Deliberation Councils in the 1970s (Koike, 1994). The massive export success that accompanied these PPD initiatives and their associated industrial policies became the natural aspiration for many Latin American countries at the time. However, the enthusiasm for replicating the experience sharply contrasted with its results (Baer, 1972).

All these policy efforts at the sector level face the challenge of high dimensionality (Hausmann, 2008): There are just too many sectors and too many relevant constraints or missing public inputs that are differentially relevant for each sector. Because of the multiple layers, governments often do not have enough information to design and implement effective policies. PPDs work as an information-revelation mechanism, helping the public sector to gather valuable information and prioritize the most relevant issues hindering productivity. The knowledge required for effective intervention can benefit from research but must go well beyond desk work and be validated by decision-makers in selected sectors.

PPDs are sector-specific initiatives for which success hinges on choosing the right sectors and identifying the correct issues to address. The modern approach to industrial policy and the logic behind PPDs is that instead of picking winners – one of the tenets of the early Korean and Japanese experience which led to the discredit of industrial policy in Latin America – sectors shall be selected by a data-driven approach and interventions should focus on solving coordination failures or providing public goods that are specific to the sectors. In that context, Productivity Task Forces in Namibia occurred during a three-year Harvard Growth Lab research project that provided vital insights for its development. First, they benefited from a thorough analysis of the industrial ecosystem of Namibia and a roadmap of export diversification opportunities that could be pursued by redeploying existing skills and productive capacities (Hausmann et al., 2022). Second, a comprehensive growth diagnostic exercise was performed that provided some priors regarding the potential constraints to productivity for the median industry in Namibia. These inputs were meant to inform the identification of constraints, which in turn would help PPDs. Far too often, PPDs prioritize market interventions, such as subsidies, barriers to trade, or tax relief to compensate for them. The exercise resulted in an in-depth comparative analysis of all production factors that was also a valuable input to complement the discussions and deliberations at the PPD table. These inputs are meant to inform the identification of sectors and constraints but were validated with domestic government and private sector stakeholders.

The goal of the Government of Namibia in launching the PPD initiative – Productivity Task Forces – was to spur competitiveness and exports in selected sectors by fostering a collaborative environment where public and private stakeholders can jointly tackle productivity constraints. As we will see in the next section, that purpose in itself represented a significant challenge to the status quo and the historical legacy of apartheid experienced by Namibia prior to independence (1990). By increasing productivity and competitiveness at the sector level, the government also meant to diversify its sources of foreign currency, stabilize its balance of payments deficit, and create formal jobs for Namibians.

This study provides a comprehensive analysis of Namibia's experience with its first Productivity Task Force focused on the high-value fruits sector. Section 2 provides background context preceding the implementation of Productivity Task Forces, documents previous efforts to set PPDs in Namibia, summarizes the key takeaways from the Growth Diagnostic exercise that preceded and informed the PPD (Hausmann et al., 2022), and presents valuable lessons incorporated into the design and implementation of Productivity Task Forces. Section 3 presents an overview of the planning stage leading up to launching the high-value fruits task force. We reflect on the experience of building a functional and coordinated team, selecting a sector to kick-start the dialogs, and preliminary work essential for launching the dialogs. Section 4 describes the process of running the task force. Productivity Task Forces are meant to be a problem-solving mechanism. To illustrate that process, we organized this section around each of the productivity constraints identified during the first meetings. Section 5 provides an assessment of the impact of the task force both in the public and in the private sectors. Section 6 takes stock of reflections and lessons learned from this case study.

2 The Context of Productivity Task Forces in Namibia

In its thirty years since independence, Namibia has been characterized by an overreliance on mineral resources, procyclicality of macroeconomic policy, and significant income disparities. After an initial decade marked by nation-building and slow growth (1990–2000), the Namibian economy embarked on a rapid growth acceleration that extended over fifteen years (2000–2015) within the context of the global commodity super cycle. Favorable terms of trade translated into an investment and export boom in the mining sector, amplified in the economy's non-tradable sector through a massive government spending spree. From 2008 onward, the Namibian record of fiscal discipline was relaxed, with public expenditure going from 25% to 44% of gross domestic product (GDP) and the fiscal balance moving from a surplus of 6.6% of GDP to a deficit of 8.6% between 2008 and 2016. The provision of essential public goods expanded rapidly, with significant improvements in enrollment rates at all education levels, access to health facilities and electricity in urban and rural areas, and quality of infrastructure in roads, ports, railways, and airport access.

As the commodity super cycle ended, Namibia experienced a substantial economic reversal. With debt-to-GDP ratios 3.5 times higher than those in 2008, the country embarked on a fiscal consolidation effort. Investment and exports plummeted. Output in the mining sector continued to rise, but without the fiscal impulse, the non-tradable sector entered a deep recession. By 2020, the primary balance had been brought back to equilibrium, but the financial burden of debt kept the fiscal accounts in deficit. Overall, Namibia went from growing at a compounded annual growth rate (CAGR) of 3.1% on average over the 2000–2015 expansion to contracting by 2.1% between 2015 and 2019 – a total loss of 8.1% in income per capita in just four years. At this point, Covid-19 hit, undoing the fiscal adjustment Namibia had painstakingly engineered. The economy contracted an additional 6.6% of GDP in 2020 and has been gradually recovering since – against a robust fiscal consolidation process.

Inequality has been endemic throughout Namibia's history and is reflected across the population's demographics and geography. At present, most Namibians cannot access well-paying formal sector jobs, as these tend to be particularly scarce outside of the public sector. Looking forward, the road to inclusive growth and broad prosperity entails expanding the formal private labor market by diversifying the Namibian economy – within the fiscal consolidation context, growth must come from exports and investments associated with exports – while at the same time removing the barriers preventing Namibians from accessing these opportunities inherited from the apartheid era.

2.1 The Most Binding Constraints for the Median Industry

In 2020, the Growth Lab at Harvard University partnered with the Government of Namibia to produce research-based inputs for a policy strategy aimed at promoting sustainable and inclusive growth. Within the context of the research initiative, the Growth Lab team developed a Growth Diagnostic aimed at identifying the most binding constraints to productivity and investment for the median tradable sector in the country forces (Hausmann et al., 2022). These efforts are relevant for the PPDs at the sector level, as they provide priors regarding potential binding constraints firms in selected sectors might face. The results of this exercise shall inform the PPD but would not have the final word regarding which are the most critical issues to address: There might be constraints that are relevant for a particular sector that do not constrain the median sector, as well as constraints for the median sector that are not relevant for a particular sector.

The Growth Diagnostic of Namibia identified three binding constraints. From a knowledge agglomeration standpoint, Namibia was missing the productive capabilities and skills necessary to sustain long periods of growth and create good jobs. The low degree of know-how agglomeration inferred from its productive structure – gathered by the Economic Complexity Index (ECI) – left little opportunities for diversification that could be pursued by redeploying existing skills. As the marginal cost of acquiring new capabilities at low levels of agglomeration tends to be high, the government needed to take a more active role in sorting coordination and information failures associated with productive diversification and self-discovery. Public–private dialogs at the sector level might be the cornerstone of a diversification strategy by identifying missing inputs or coordination problems that affect the productivity of existing industries and designing and implementing interventions to address them.

A shortage of specialized skills also constrains Namibia's growth prospects – three empirical facts derived from research based on Labor Force Surveys pointed in this direction. First, there were significant wage premiums in skill-intensive industries and occupations. Second, highly educated and experienced workers faced the lowest unemployment rates by a considerable margin. Third, skill-intensive industries were growing at a rate considerably lower than the rest of the economy. Skill shortage seemed to be constraining not only existing industries but also the development of new engines of growth, limiting access to opportunities for Namibians across all skill levels. Missing skills at the top of the spectrum depressed job creation at the bottom. The evidence suggests that highly skilled foreigners tend to function as complements – rather than substitutes – to Namibian workers: industries with larger shares of high-skill workers tend to pay low-skill workers significantly higher wages.

Lastly, policy uncertainty was reported to hinder productivity, economic diversification, and foreign talent attraction. Existing levels of policy uncertainty – instability or absence of appropriate regulations, worries about potential issues associated with property rights, inefficiencies, or biases in the ruling of domestic courts – might not deter investments in resource-based industries but might be a hurdle for other types of industries, especially the ones that have a choice regarding their international location. A simpler and more transparent investment environment might be necessary to attract these investments, complemented with a more comprehensive set of international investment protection treaties.

These constraints are a great starting point for PPDs, as they provide general priors on what might be preventing a typical or median firm from being more competitive. They inform the efforts of the sponsoring entity and supply rigorous and data-driven inputs that can be used to kick-start the dialog and set the tone for the meetings, where they shall be discussed and validated by participants on Productivity Task Forces (PTF) at the sector level.

2.2 Previous Public–Private Dialogs

Most developing countries have experimented with PPDs in some form. Whether these efforts were focused on specific sectors, on issues that cut across different economic activities, or much broader matters affecting the general investment climate, it is crucial to take stock of the country's previous experience and try to incorporate as many learnings as possible within the policy design.

In the case of Namibia, there were some efforts to launch PPD at the sector level in 2012, sponsored by the Ministry of Industrialization and Trade (MIT). The date of launching of this first precursor of PTFs came somewhat late – even considering that Namibia just got its independence in 1990 – a feature that can be attributed to the distrust between the public and the private sector, derived from the legacy of exclusion of apartheid. "We simply do not have a culture or background that is propense to public-private dialogs."[1]

In particular, the convening party within the MTI was the Namibian Trade Forum (NTF), an entity created in 2010 with the mandate to become "the indispensable PPD platform for a conducive business environment" by "influencing trade policy and economic development."[2] The first wave of PPD was launched in four economic sectors: Agriculture, fisheries, services, and manufacturing. These four would be followed shortly by the Local Authorities Dialog, a series of PPD for Urban and Rural Development, were the NTF acted as an intermediary between the government and local community leaders. Interestingly, the dialogs were recorded as part of the MIT PPD initiative, despite not having private firms explicitly involved. A second wave of PPD brought together government officials at the MIT with private sector representatives from Business and Finance Services; Information, Communication, and Technology (ICT); Transportation and Logistics; Tourism, and Energy. The meetings did not have a pre-established frequency. Still, they met whenever the NTF considered it appropriate or had recorded enough progress on a particular issue to report to the group.

We have not been able to document how long these series of PPDs were held. From our interviews with officials at the MTI, NTF, and private sector representatives, we understand that the ones holding on for longer were those focused on fisheries and agriculture. In the former case, the dialogs were carried out at the level of a committee formed by a confederation of Namibian fisheries. In the case of agriculture, the list of participants suggests that the convention was

---

[1] Interview with Ndiitah Nghipondoka-Robiati, Deputy Executive Director and Permanent Secretary at Ministry of Industrialization and Trade, and Stacey Pinto, CEO of the Namibia Trade Forum; June 10, 2021.

[2] See the website of the Namibia Trade Forum: www.ntf.org.na. Consulted on November 14, 2022.

much broader, including officials from the Ministry of Agriculture, representatives from labor unions, agricultural boards across the country, and a few private sector firms.

Despite the broad scope of the NTF mission and the wide range of Simultaneous dialogs in place, the fact that the NTF hosted these PPDs did influence the type of issues raised by the private sector participants, which were primarily focused on trade regulations and market access. Either because the mandate received by these PPDs was narrow or because participants were prone to bring up issues where the convening authority had some direct influence, the fact remains that most of the problems were related to international trade, such as access to foreign markets, tariff, and nontariff barriers, import and export quotas.

Naturally, most of the matters where progress was recorded across these PPDs belong to the realm of action of the MTI. When issues such as skill shortages and government arrears were raised, MTI officials were forced to reach out to other public entities to address them. It is here that the PPD lost some traction. Impatient at the slow pace of progress, private sector representatives started reaching out to government officials outside the scope of PPD, ultimately undermining the PPD initiative. "We were not recognized as a legitimate channel in areas out of trade; because of that, firms always were looking for plan B by appealing and lobbying directly to government officials in other entities outside the scope of the PDD and the NTF."[3]

The experience of the PPD in the agricultural sector seems to be particularly informative. First, the government held various types of PPD simultaneously for different industries within agriculture. Labor unions, agrarian boards, and firms switched from one initiative to the next, looking for the most effective one. Second, the initiatives often included a broad array of actors that did not have common ground and, thereby, were affected by different types of constraints. While large farmers were mainly focused on the availability of fertile land and skill shortages (difficulties in attracting and retaining qualified labor), small farmers were more concerned about transportation costs, lack of scale, irregular quality of inputs and products, and other logistic issues that prevented them from reaching the shelves of Namibian stores. Finally, the large number of representatives on the different agricultural PPD initiatives organized by the government granted a broad representation of the sector – perhaps too broad – that came at the cost of lower functionality and overall operating efficiency. Eventually, once the trade and market access issues were sorted, the PPD lost relevance and faded away in time.

---

[3] Interview with Ndiitah Nghipondoka-Robiati, Deputy Executive Director and Permanent Secretary at Ministry of Industrialization and Trade, and Stacey Pinto, CEO of the Namibia Trade Forum; June 10, 2021.

2.3 Lessons Learned

First, the choice of the entity that convenes and leads the PPD tends to predetermine the type of constraints and roadblocks that surface. In the case of Namibia, the choice of the NTF and the specific mandate issued by the government restricted the policy space to issues associated with international trade and trade regulations, not necessarily because they were the most relevant but rather because participants perceived that was the policy area where the convening entity had the most influence. Finding a convening entity with the authority to mobilize other public officials would contribute to streamlining and consolidating the platform of PPD as the mechanism to identify and address constraints to productivity at the sector level.

Second, there should be a period of experimentation, evaluation, and adaptation to tailor the initiative to the specific context of the place before expanding it more broadly. In the case of the PPD launched by MIT from 2012 onwards, the initial plan seems to have been too ambitious, incorporating at least eight different economic sectors in a short period. A more parsimonious process would have entailed choosing a pilot sector, learning from experience, contextualizing the initiative, and expanding to other sectors. That would have also allowed authorities to create momentum around the progress of the pilot PPD, recording some early success that would then increase the incentives of private entrepreneurs in other sectors to demand the constitution of an effective dialog and participate actively.

Third, in structuring PPDs, it is vital to strike the right balance between representation and functionality. The experience of the PPD in agriculture seems to have incorporated a broad arrange of actors – different sizes of farming units, labor unions, agricultural boards, plus several government dependencies including the Ministry of Agriculture and MTI – that enhanced their representativeness, potentially at the cost of lower functionality and efficiency. PPD should be an effective vehicle to promote collective thinking among informed parties on what is constraining productivity at the sector level, analyze the policy space in search of interventions that help alleviate or mitigate the constraints, assign responsibilities, and follow up on execution. The size of the PPD should be broad enough to include relevant parties likely to be affected by the same constraints but small enough to guarantee that the group remains functional from an execution standpoint. Ultimately, the goal is to identify a set of constraints hindering the competitiveness of all firms in the sector and develop effective interventions to address them for the benefit of all firms in the industry and not only those sitting at the PPD.

Finally, it is essential to establish an appropriate periodicity in the meetings of sectoral PPD while also considering the policy and political context. The irregular periods between PPD at the NTF may have mirrored a context were mobilizing resources and implementing policy interventions happen slowly. While it is essential to factor this into the PPD policy design to avoid organizing unnecessary meetings, the fact that periodicity was not established ex ante also created a lot of uncertainty and detracted structure, accountability, and predictability from the policy initiative.

3 Setting Up the Task Force

The process of setting up the task force in Namibia did not start from scratch. The Harvard Growth Lab proposed the idea to the Government of Namibia as part of a series of policy efforts to spur productivity and competitiveness while diversifying exports away from the traditional engines of growth. This proposal was based on previous international experiences, especially the Peruvian *Mesas Ejecutivas* (ME). As Ghezzi (2017) explains, PPDs or MEs are an efficient way of dealing with coordination problems in middle-income countries where demand for coordination is increasing as the economic development path becomes more and more complex. Catering to the growing relevance of coordination problems requires (1) a private sector that is constructive, proactive, and willing to work with government to solve problems, (2) a public sector able to mobilize around specific issues and deliver, and (3) Political authority with a convening capacity to bring different stakeholders together, resolve disputes or propose major policy changes.

PPD typically have two levels of participants (Ghezzi, 2017): ground-level and high-level bodies. The ground level comprises participants in both sectors who are knowledgeable about the specifics of the sector, in addition to the entity hosting and facilitating the dialog. The private sector representatives are protagonists in the discussion because they have specific knowledge about the issues that must be addressed. On the other hand, public sector representatives must have the capacity to understand and mobilize resources to contribute with problem-solving by providing missing public inputs or correcting market failures. There are occasions in which the working group reaches a gridlock because the solutions proposed go beyond the capacity of the public sector participants and require political support from higher levels of authority, which is when the high-level body comes to action. In turn, the team coordinating the PPD takes care of the overall functioning of the group, organizing and hosting the meetings, developing research to inform the problems discussed and avenues for action, support the group in identifying options, assign responsibilities and following up with execution.

The steps taken to set up the PTF in Namibia followed a similar process. More specifically:

1. Secure the political authorization necessary to organize the meetings and mobilize public sector entities to address the issues brought up in the dialogs.
2. Identify the government entity that will act as convener.
3. Establish a team dedicated within the chosen entity to organize and operate the PTF.
4. Define a data-driven list of sectors or factors of production with significant potential to deliver export growth (tradable sectors).
5. Develop background research and organize preliminary meetings with stakeholders from potential sectors or factors of production.
6. Select a sector as a target of the first PTF that would work as a pilot to learn from implementation and gradually contextualize the dialogs.
7. Develop some background research to identify a preliminary list of barriers or issues to be address that will be later validated with stakeholders at the table.

In this section, we document the process of setting up the PTF in Namibia in three blocks, comprising these seven steps: (i) building the team running the task force, (ii) selecting the sector to kick-start the task force, and (iii) preliminary work that needs to be done before kick-off.

3.1 Building the Team: Political Champions and Policy Officers

The launch of the PTFs as part of a broader effort to diversify the economy was approved by an authorizing environment comprising three institutions within the Namibian government: The Ministry of Finance (represented by the Minister Iipumbu Shiimi), the National Planning Commission (represented by its highest authority, Obeth Kandjoze), and the Central Bank of Namibia (represented by its Deputy Governor, Ebson Uanguta). As part of the approval process, the group had to decide the government entity that would host PTFs and facilitate the dialogs. It was not an easy choice.

While some of the initial candidates proposed were not a good fit from a functional standpoint and were discarded with relative ease (the Ministry of Finance, the National Planning Commission), the Ministry of Industrialization and Trade held a more legitimate aspiration as the precursor of PPDs in Namibia. However, the learnings derived from the previous experience and the authorities' desire to relaunch these dialogs, increasing their effectiveness and expanding the scope of issues they could potentially tackle, led to an intense discussion that delayed the implementation of PTFs for a few months.

One natural candidate was the Namibian Investment and Development Board (NIPDB). The NIPDB had been created in 2019 as a nonprofit organization incorporated under Section 21 of the Companies Act (28 of 2004). Placed at the Office of the President of Namibia, it was entitled with the mission of attracting foreign direct investment, promoting productive diversification, and spurring the creation of formal jobs in the private sector. To accomplish that purpose, it was key that the entity developed the capacity to perform background research and establish a constructive dialog with private sector of companies present in Namibia (intensive margin) and abroad (extensive margin), to identify and address industry-specific barriers to productivity and competitiveness. There were obvious advantages of the NIPDB over other government entities, and more particularly the Namibian Trade Forum at the Minister of Industrialization and Trade. First, it was a new organization that could recast the PPD effort and frame it within a more relevant context for the development of Namibia. Second, it was registered as an autonomous entity responding directly to the Presidency but was not subject to the limitations of government entities, allowing them to offer better working conditions thereby improving its capacity to attract talent. And third, it had a relatively small, yet flexible, structure. These characteristics made NIDPB the right institution for running the task force because they freed it from other institutions' bureaucratic hurdles.

Based on these advantages, the three institutions comprising the authorizing environment presented and got approval from Cabinet to appoint the NIPDB as the host of PTFs in Namibia.

The approval from Cabinet and the backing from three institutions with significant leverage within the Namibian government and the overall political establishment was one of the key factors behind the successful launch of the PTFs. To run the dialogs, the NIPDB needed a dedicated team, and the administrative capacity required to organize and lead the meetings, follow-up on specific topics, identify loopholes, and push for solutions.

The authorizing environment helped to source the funding needed to secure those capacities and played a pivotal role in the convening of the PTFs and the mobilization of other public entities to address the issues raised by participants. The presence of one of the key representatives – Minister of Finance, Iipumbu Shiimi – as head of the meetings provided a significant impulse to the launching and conveyed to private sector participants the political support to the effort and its importance for the Government of Namibia.

However, a team comprising solely high-level officials would have the political support to undertake any policy reform but would lack the technical or administrative capacity to identify the right constraints for the sector, design policies to address them, and coordinate the process of change. On the other hand, technical teams might lack decision-making power, thus making it impossible for them to make things happen. At the time, the overall reflection was that the right team should have a mix of both features, that is, senior officials who understand politics (champions) and mid-level and junior officials who can identify policy reforms and coordinate with multiple stakeholders (policy officers).

3.1.1 Champions and Political Support

The participation of champions (high-level political agents) in the task force was essential during the first meetings. The Minister of Finance of Namibia played this role for the high-value fruits task force. Without the presence of a high-level authority from government, it would have been much more difficult to create momentum around the effort and convey the willingness of government to address the barriers to competitiveness. He was joined by other high-level figures from the Namibian government who belonged to the authorizing environment or were summoned because of their relevance to the issues being discussed (for instance, the Ministry of Agriculture). Also, representatives from different ministries or government areas often needed direct political validation to move forward with policy solutions identified in the task force, and the presence of the high-level authorities made that easier.

Early during the PTF, the team realized that solving productivity constraints implied changing policies, which could mean implementing new programs or working to improve existing ones. In both cases, the political champions were essential to move forward. For example, when policy change did not imply creating new programs but improving existing practices, the champions provided support to reform government areas that needed improvement. In Namibia's high-value task force, one of the constraints identified was the lack of a competent phytosanitary authority. The officials of the Ministry of Agriculture, Water, and Land Reform (MAWLR) were not entirely aware of the negative impacts of not having a capable phytosanitary authority on exports, thus were not making it a priority to strengthen that area.

In other cases, policy change implies solving complex political issues that require political consensus or legislative reform. In the case of the high-value fruits PTF in Namibia, one of the issues the farmers raised was their capacity to access land in regions with a communal land tenure system. Until 1990, the population of Namibia experienced forced displacement and land expropriation during apartheid. In 1990, the country inherited a distribution of land in which agricultural land ownership was concentrated in a white minority (Melber, 2005). As part of a resettlement policy that aimed to recover the land rights for the Namibian population, the government enacted the Agricultural (Commercial) Land Reform Act in 1995. The land question has remained a highly sensitive political issue in Namibia. Most commercial farmers are white, including those in the high-value fruits task force. Thus, moving forward with reforms in such a politically sensitive area was unfeasible for the technical teams at the PTF.

Policy changes require political support when improving existing programs and solving complex political issues. The political champions in the PTF provided the support and decision-making authority needed to move forward. They became instrumental in directing discussions to bridge the gaps between different viewpoints. Ultimately, the champions were extremely helpful in nudging the alignment between stakeholders and mobilizing public sector entities. On one hand, public sector stakeholders had strong political views on specific areas that prevented them from considering evidence-based perspectives. On the other hand, private sector stakeholders insisted on driving the discussion toward the need for more government support in the form of transfers or land instead of focusing on barriers to productivity. In both cases, the champions provided the leadership required to reach a consensus, identify the right issues and their potential solutions, and move forward with implementation issues.

The political champion who motorized the initiative of PTFs in Namibia complemented political authority with management skills and technical knowledge. Minister Iipumbu Shiimi was not only able to get political support from the cabinet to kick-start the pilot of PTFS and convene different stakeholders but was also efficient in moving the project forward and bringing key government officials to work on different policy areas. On top of that, he also had a solid background in economics, which ended up being an outstanding contribution to the discussions. He did not participate in all meetings, but his involvement during the launching and the initial steps of the process was essential for the success of the pilot. In 2024, Minister Shiimi was named Africa's top-performing Minister of Finance of the Year by the African Banker Awards during the African Development Bank Group Annual Meetings (African Banker Awards, 2024).

3.1.2 Policy Officers and Administrative Capabilities

Identifying productivity constraints requires a mix of technical expertise, policymaking skills, and contextual knowledge. The participants from the private sector usually have the incentives to ask for government actions that help them increase their profits or rents. It is not practical or reasonable to ask the private sector to internalize social and political goals into their objective function. The team in charge of running the task force faces the challenge of filtering private sector proposals so that they are (i) politically supportable, (ii) administratively feasible, and (iii) technically correct. The first criterion often falls under the capacity of the political champions; the latter two are tasked to the policy officers.

When pursuing administratively feasible ideas, the PTF team's main challenge was navigating the government structure. In Namibia, the task force officers needed a practical understanding of how the government works to identify feasible policy solutions. The NIPDB team thoroughly understood the government's political system and inner workings. Although this might seem a simple requirement, it is often the case that government structures in developing countries include many informal procedures. This implies that policy officers do not have a priori clear map of what needs to be done and who is ultimately responsible for implementing a specific policy change. In Namibia, the government's political structure and informal practices are less complex than in other countries because of the country's relatively small size (it is more likely that everyone knows each other). In addition, the South-West Africa People's Organization (SWAPO) has been the ruling party since independence, resulting in a relatively consistent political structure.

Understanding the political and governmental system was essential for extending invitations to public sector stakeholders to participate in the PTF meetings. Ultimately, the PTF core team was not in charge of implementing solutions but rather ensuring that the relevant public sector offices addressed the issues identified in the meetings. One of the primary skills the NIPDB team had to strengthen to develop a successful PTF was "follow-up capacity." There is no secret sauce in the capacity to follow up effectively, as it is a matter of continuously organizing a defined and practical agenda. However, even when it is not complex or technical, it could be a skill in shortage, depending on the context. The NIPDB team quickly realized that their ability to follow up with public sector officers and define a constructive and effective agenda was the cornerstone of success.

The policy officers running the task force also needed a toolkit to assess the technical soundness of proposals. The NIPDB team that coordinated the PTFs in Namibia had the analytical skills needed to perform that job and benefited from having the Growth Diagnostic of Namibia developed by the Harvard Growth Lab. For example, the diagnostic can help in informing how appropriate requests for tax breaks or subsidies are; market interventions often come at the expense of the industry's competitiveness or are not geared toward improving productivity (but usually compensate for other factors hindering competitiveness).

3.2 Selecting the Initial Sector: High-Value Fruits

During the first half of 2021, the Minister of Finance got approval from the Cabinet to start a pilot of productivity task forces on a sector to be selected. The NIPDB core team started working on the PTF pilot in July 2021. The first discussions about sector selection happened after a few introductory meetings to get the NIPBD team acquainted with the notion of productivity task forces – goals, structuring, steps, methodology – during which the Harvard Growth Lab and NIPDB exchanged ideas on how to approach the project and the best way to contextualize it to Namibia. Once the basics were covered, the team moved to sector selection process, which followed a two-step process: (i) analysis of industries according to their growth potential and feasibility, and (ii) joint selection of a sector based on a combination of quantitatively and qualitative criteria, contextual knowledge, and learning by doing.

3.2.1 Growth Potential and Feasibility: High-Value Fruits versus Other Candidates

The first question was about the role of sector selection within the context of a broader national diversification strategy. There was no need to delay the task force setup until a thorough and research-heavy review of the development and diversification strategies was done. As a pilot, the purpose was to get the initiative started on a sector with significant potential but not politically controversial, allowing experimentation and adaptation to contextualize the process and give PTF firmer ground before expanding to other sectors. However, as mentioned in Section 2, Namibia's political leadership had reviewed its long-term development strategy and created a certain degree of consensus over the pathways to inclusive and sustainable economic growth. In that context, the government decided to work with Harvard's Growth Lab in developing ways of addressing the constraints identified in the Growth Diagnostics (Hausmann et al., 2022) and diversifying the economy based on the Economic Complexity Report (Hausmann et al., 2022). Namibia's low levels of knowledge agglomeration and scarce opportunities for productive diversification implied that working in relatively well-established sectors would yield more realistic returns in the short term than focusing on more complex yet less feasible industries that were part of a longer-term diversification strategy. The PTF started with the high-value fruits sector, which is comprised of low-complexity products near Namibia's productive capabilities. Figure 1 shows that products comprised within this category – grapes, dates, and berries – were less complex and more feasible than most products recommended in the economic complexity report (Hausmann et al., 2022).

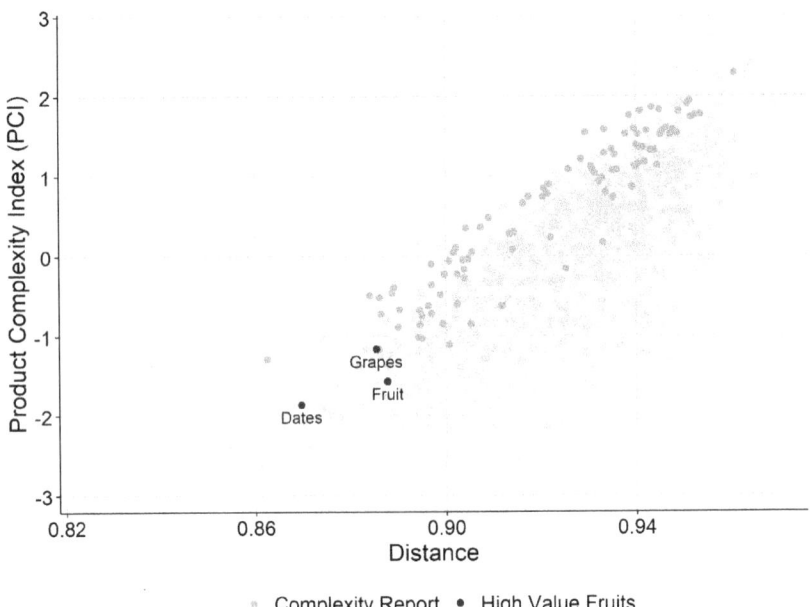

Figure 1 Namibia's diversification opportunities
Source: International trade data from Atlas of Economic Complexity (2019)

The NIPDB team developed a preliminary list of sectors that could be the focus of the PTF pilot. The list was discussed in a few meetings, but the process of preliminary research and discussion was not long. The priority was to get started and not to develop a comprehensive understanding of the sectors. The options under consideration were:

- A manufacturing industry like the automotive or food industries of beverages, processed meat, and dairy products.
- Cosmetics industry of products like Marula oil
- Fishing industry
- High-value fruits (grapes, dates and berries)

The problem with most manufacturing industries was that they tended to show high levels of market concentration, as highlighted during the initial meetings. However, this was the case for most sectors in Namibia, which is a small economy with a population of only 2.5 million, where most industries have a small number of players that constitute monopolies or small oligopolies with significant market power. This feature led to a discussion on whether the characteristics of the Namibian economy justified an adaptation to the PTF principles to work in sectors with fewer players than previous documented experiences. It would not have been an issue if the PTF had operated at the sector level rather than exclusively for the dominant player. If that were the case, the process would facilitate firm entry by alleviating constraints that currently deter potential investors.

Although market concentration levels were a concern, the main reason for shifting the focus away from manufacturing industries was that the other candidates with significant growth potential were considered more adjacent– within a closer range of Namibia's existing skillset. Namibia is a country with low know-how agglomeration for which productive diversification would require well-targeted long jumps (Hausmann et al., 2022). Several manufacturing industries considered in the initial list of sectors, like the automotive industry, represented broader skill gaps than other more realistic choices for a PTF pilot. Ultimately, the runners-up showing signs of attractive economic growth potential were cosmetics, fishing, and high-value fruits. The three had comparative advantages in Namibia and were underperforming relative to their potential.

The cosmetics industry, which included a manufacturing component, presented itself as a feasible and attractive candidate. The sector showed good coordination levels as it organized the Namibian Network of the Cosmetics Industry (NANCi). The NIPDB team was already supporting the cosmetics businesses in accessing international markets, as they saw a large potential for them if they managed to tap into global markets and growing international demand. L'Oréal, the largest cosmetics company in the world, had documented a growth rate of 8% in 2021 for the global market, which went well and above a mere recovery from the pandemic and continued in 2022 (6%) and 2023 (8%). The expectation was that the market would continue growing as fast as the expansion of the global middle class and rising demand from Asia (L'Oréal, 2023). Some Namibian cosmetics businesses started exporting to European and North American markets, like Taneta Investment, a small business established in 2015 that developed cosmetic oils based on Marula, a fruit indigenous to the Southern African region (US Embassy Windhoek, 2022). In turn, revenues in the South African cosmetics sector have continuously grown in the past decade due to growing domestic demand and investments in local capabilities. In 2016 L'Oréal opened its first Research & Innovation Center in South Africa (InvestSA, 2020). In summary, the economic growth potential of the Namibian cosmetics industry was promising, positioning it as a strong contender for the first PTF.

The main factor against the cosmetics industry was that it comprised primarily small and medium-sized enterprises (SMEs). While this was not necessarily problematic, it did imply a steeper learning curve for achieving economies of scale compared to industries with companies already benefiting from access to capital, markets, and higher operational efficiency. Developing a PTF focused on a sector comprised of SMEs was a possibility. As in the case of highly concentrated markets, the PTF could be tailored to address the specific challenges these businesses face. However, other sectors demonstrated greater economies of scale, making them more attractive for the first pilot: solving productivity problems in these sectors could potentially have higher economic impacts in the short term, which would signal the PTF's effectiveness as a policy tool and provide momentum to expand the initiative to other sectors.

Of all the candidates initially considered, fishing and high-value fruits were the two candidates with the highest short-term growth potential for the first PTF. In the case of the former, worldwide revenues and the production volume for processed and fresh products have sharply increased since the end of the pandemic (Statista, 2024). However, prices for fishing products had also increased between 2021 and 2023, suggesting that the surge in production was lower that of demand (Statista, 2024). For a fishing country like Namibia, the strong signal of a rise in demand for fishing products pointed to significant room to increase its exports.

As the FAO (2023b) reported, Namibia boasts some of the most productive fishing grounds globally. This productivity is primarily attributed to the cold Benguela current, which fosters an exceptionally favorable ecosystem. Fishing is a critical industry in Namibia, consistently contributing around 3% to the nation's GDP since 2007 (USA ITA, 2024) and accounting for over 10% of total annual exports from 2000 to 2018 (Atlas of Economic Complexity). The exports of fish products in Namibia consistently increased at an annual compounded growth rate of over 3% between the early 2000s and 2013, when they peaked. They stagnated between 2013 and 2019, a period of worldwide slowdown of international export growth. Yet after 2019, the fishing industry experienced a dramatic export collapse: over 35% between 2019 and 2021 (Figure 2).

Namibia's fish exports declined following a political scandal that surfaced on November 12, 2019, while the discussion to select the pilot sector was at full speed. On that day, WikiLeaks released what came to be known as the Fishrot Files, a trove of thousands of documents and email exchanges from employees of Samherji, one of Iceland's leading fish industry companies (Dell, 2023; Fabricius, 2022; Henley, 2019). These documents revealed that the company had allegedly paid hundreds of millions to senior politicians and officials in Namibia to secure the country's valuable fishing quotas. The total value of suspicious transactions was estimated at US$ 650 million (IPPR & Transparency International Iceland, 2022). Samherji finalized its operations in Namibia shortly after that. The scandal was a major reputational hit for the Namibian fishing industry, with thousands of fishermen losing their jobs (IPPR & Transparency International Iceland, 2022).

Public–Private Dialog and Productivity 21

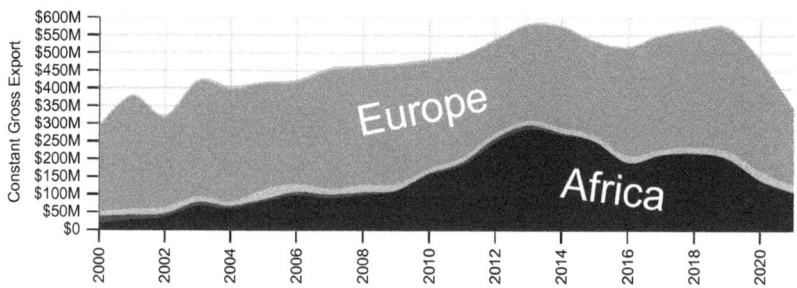

Figure 2 Namibia's exports of fish products (2000–2021)
Source: Atlas of Economic Complexity

Ultimately, the political controversy surrounding Namibia's fishing industry was a significant drawback for it being considered the first sector for the PTF. Being at the center of public and political attention would not have given the room necessary to experiment and adapt that was necessary to contextualize the initiative to the particularities of Namibia, one of the key goals of the launching of the pilot sector.

At last, the high-value fruits sector was the last one standing in the initial list. It was also a sector with clear growth potential. One way of analyzing the prospects of a sector is to look at whether it has comparative advantages and, at the same time, is underperforming its competitors in other countries. In Peru, for example, the *Mesas Ejecutivas* started with the forestry sector. This sector had a series of comparative advantages yet was underperforming vis-à-vis other countries (Ghezzi, 2017), which suggested the presence of several constraints affecting its competitiveness. In Namibia, the same fundamental reason guided the narrowing down of candidates, which ultimately led to the high-value fruits sector. Along with the meat industry, Namibia's high-value fruits sector is the most export-oriented industry within the agriculture sector. According to FAO production estimates, table grapes were 70% of fruit production in 2020 in Namibia. Yet grapes, dates, and blueberry production were relatively new in Namibia. Grape growers have constantly increased their exports since they started in 2000, though they have declined since 2014 (Figure 3). On the other hand, date producers started exporting significant amounts of produce in 2014 and had experienced a fourfold increase in exports by 2019 (Figure 4). Blueberry farms are a much more recent phenomenon that started exporting in 2018.

The global demand for grapes, dates, and blueberries had been consistently increasing since the early 2000s – with growing markets in the United States, Europe, and Asia. Namibia was in an excellent position to cater to demand from the North American and European markets. The ports that can be accessed from and in

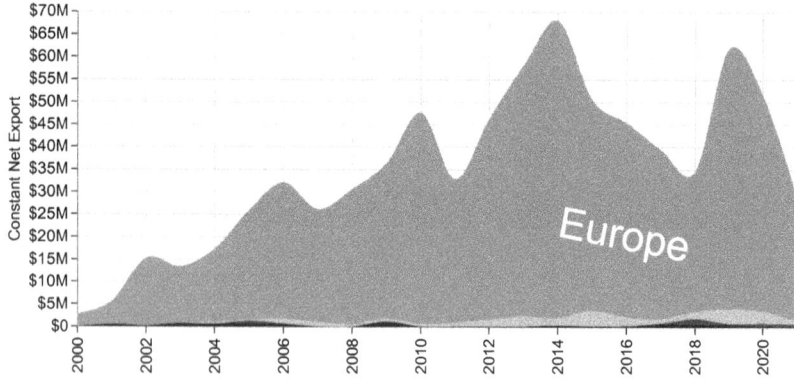

Figure 3 Namibia's exports of grapes

Source: Atlas of Economic Complexity

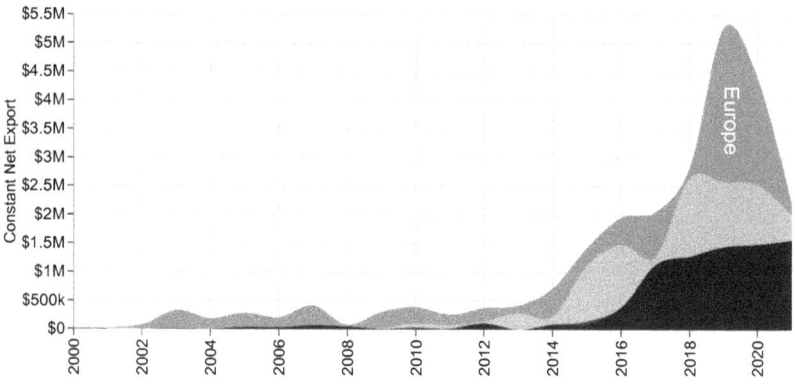

Figure 4 Namibia's exports of dates

Source: Atlas of Economic Complexity

Namibia are closer in distance to Europe than those used in leading countries in the sector, like Peru. The business of high-value fruits is highly sensitive to transportation because the less time it takes, the higher the quality of the product, as freshness is a key factor. Namibia's lower distance to Europe could be a significant comparative advantage if the country developed a competitive port infrastructure. At the time of the start of the PTF, the high-value fruit producers were utilizing the Port of Cape Town because it was closer to their farms than Walvis Bay (Namibia's main port). Nevertheless, South Africa's decline in state capacity has severely affected the performance of the Port of Cape Town, which has been decreasing positions in the global ranking of the Container Port Performance Index developed by the World Bank (Figure 5) to the point of being the worst performing port in the world in 2023 (World Bank, 2024). The inefficiencies in the Port of Cape Town

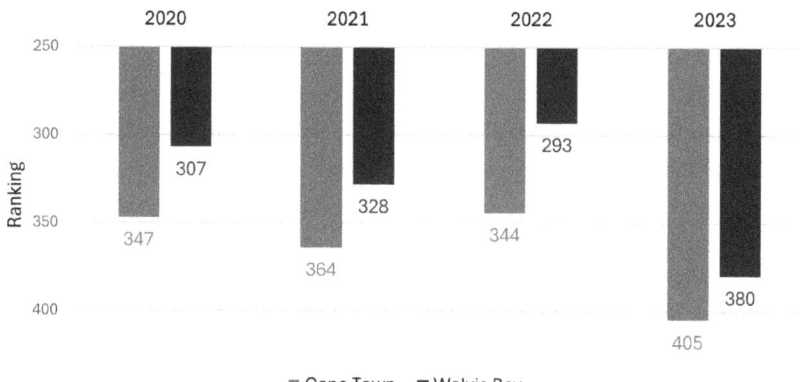

Figure 5 Container Port Performance Index of Cape Town and Walvis Bay (2020–2023)

Source: World Bank Container Port Performance Index

management have resulted in significant losses for the agriculture sector (Meintjes, 2024). Although Walvis Bay was not a peak performing port, it still ranked better than Cape Town in terms of efficiency and performance. As a result, the Namibian farmers turned to Walvis Bay as an alternative to the Cape Town port (Fresh Plaza, 2024; Meintjes, 2023).

In addition, being part of the African Growth and Opportunity Act (AGOA) gave Namibia a competitive edge when exporting to the United States vis-à-vis other non-African exporters of high-value fruits. Namibia had also established commercial relationships with multiple European countries since its independence, and, in 2014, signed an Economic Partnership Agreement with the European Union. However, the country was not in the same position to start exporting to the Asian markets, which was related to productivity constraints – as the PTF later discovered.

One of main factors that could boost Namibia's fruit exports was that its harvest season does not overlap with that of the Northern Hemisphere. Fruit harvest in Namibia spans from November to January, which offers a strategic advantage as it aligns with the off-season in major grape-producing countries in the Northern Hemisphere, including the United States and Europe. As a result, Namibian grapes can be marketed during high demand and limited supply in these regions, often commanding higher prices.

A series of domestic factors suggested the sector could take advantage of the seasonality advantage. Although access to critical inputs like water and electricity was challenging, the country had a considerable amount of underutilized land that could be allocated to high-value crops. Additionally, Namibia had the potential to compete with South Africa for investments in this sector, given the higher levels of policy uncertainty and state capacity crisis in South Africa that severely affect its investment climate. Lastly, Namibia also has a high level of unemployed working-age population, in particular in rural areas that could be recruited at competitive wages to work in agriculture.

Other factors that made the sector attractive included that Namibia imports most of its fruit consumption and the extensive land available for fruit production. As surveyed by the Namibian Agriculture Board (2023), only 4% of the produce was sourced locally in 2019, and only 17% of the total arable land was under cultivation in 2021. Furthermore, a considerable share of this land is in areas with access to water infrastructure and electricity.

In the context of this first stage, the economic analysis supporting the sector selection was necessary, but there was no need to conduct a comprehensive study of all potential sectors. Baseline desktop research was mean to feed the initial meetings, inform the discussion, and spur the conversation, but the task force itself was meant to act as an information-revelation mechanism on potential and constraints. In selecting the high-value fruits sector, a mix of political (not very sensitive or highly visible from a political standpoint), economic (significant export potential, feasibility from a skill standpoint), and industrial organizational factors (various independent players) weighed more heavily.

Box 1 The Duality of Agriculture in Namibia

Since Namibia's independence in 1990, the country has expanded farmland without significantly increasing yields, while several peer countries have experienced agricultural growth thanks to productivity gains. In the context of the Harvard Growth Lab engagement in Namibia, the research team documented that agricultural activity had grown in the previous two decades, increasing land and water use without any significant improvement in productivity. This broad pattern of land expansion under low productivity is a crucial characteristic of Namibia's agriculture sector. Another critical characteristic of the sector is its dual nature: productive agriculture in Namibia has thrived in the most arid places, whereas it struggles where water and arable land are more widely available. The sector is defined by a socioeconomic duality between the North and the South that transcends natural conditions.

The northern regions of Namibia are mostly rural yet are also the areas with the highest population density in the country. They have the lowest employment levels, highest poverty rates, and highest food insecurity.

Box 1 (cont.)

They are not on a convergence path with Namibia's economic growth centers. Most of the population in the North keeps traditional social, legal, and cultural norms, which include ways of doing subsistence agriculture, pastoralism, and food consumption habits. The norms also include a system of communal land in which the local traditional authorities assign land tenure to families or business projects. Additionally, some areas in the North benefit from access to water in a way no other region of Namibia enjoys, both through rainfall and river basins. However, they do not necessarily have the best soil in the broader region – which has high components of sand and clay. Despite having the best conditions for agriculture and the largest working-age population available for work in the country, there are no significant productive agricultural developments in the northern regions. Agriculture in the north is primarily small-scale or subsistence, and the regions remains locked in a Malthusian trap.

On the other hand, commercial agriculture thrives in the South of Namibia. The Southern regions have the lowest population density in the country and a private property system of land tenure. The low population density is a long-term effect of the Herero and Namaqua genocide carried out by the German army in 1904–1908, during the German colonization of Namibia (Melber, 2014). Additionally, white Afrikaners have developed extensive farms in the South, whereas they don't have access to land in the North. Unsurprisingly, most high-value fruit farms (grapes and dates) are in the South.

3.2.2 A Checklist for Sector Selection

The discussion about selecting the sector to kick start the first PTF highlighted that the growth and export potential of Namibia's high-value fruits industry made it a compelling candidate. Nevertheless, the most vital points in favor of the sector were the ones described next. These came up as a checklist of features the PTF in Namibia should have, given previous experiences in PPDs in the country.

The scope of the sector. The sector was comprised by a set of firms with similar characteristics affected by a well-defined set of shared constraints. Although this might seem simple, it can be a complex feature depending on the sector. It is easy to define the issues common to the firms within the forestry sector but hard to understand those to firms in the mining value chain – which can do very different types of things (e.g., mining services, mining machinery, and mining extraction). The high-value fruits sector had a clear set of problems which had driven farmers to organize themselves. The industry was also broad enough to include diverse firms producing different crops in different parts of the country (blueberries in the north; dates and grapes in the south). It was also broad enough to potentially include other crops not being produced in Namibia at the time or produced at a low scale, such as citrus, bananas, or mangoes. By sorting the barriers to productivity for high-value fruit farms one may be also releasing constraints for other type of fruits or products.

Market competition. As mentioned earlier, Namibia's economy is more concentrated than other economies with larger populations. As it tends to happen in small economies, it has a few conglomerates that cater to different markets and developed businesses in multiple industries. In larger countries, market competition would be a natural criterion for sector selection. Market competition is not a priority for sector selection in a country like Namibia, which has high economic concentration levels. Nevertheless, the existence of smaller players should be considered a necessary factor to account for: The high-value fruits sector included two large players but several medium-sized farmers. There must be some degree of diversity to avoid setting up a task force tailored to the needs of a few firms or a conglomerate.

Self-organization and cohesion. For the success of the task forces, there has to be a constructive set of private sectors partners that exhibit some form of organization and cohesion driven by shared problems and challenges. This was the case of the high-value fruits sector in Namibia. The NIPDB core team was cautious about selecting a sector that was neither too new nor too fragmented, as this would have made reaching a consensus more challenging. In contrast, the relatively high level of cohesion within the chosen sector facilitated the identification of initial issues, as there was widespread agreement among the farmers. Additionally, a key consideration was the direct involvement of producers in their organizations, without the creation of third-party entities like commercial chambers. Such third-party organizations can be problematic, as they tend to be selected to perform lobbying functions (with emphasis in market interventions such as protection, subsidies or tax relief) and lack the specific knowledge of the day-to-day operations and decision-making that facilitates the identification and characterization of true barriers to productivity and competitiveness.

Constructive attitude. During the first introductory meetings, it was key that the participants showed an open attitude and willingness to discuss their problems with the government within the context of the task force and explore their potential solutions. They sent a signal that they were willing to challenge their priors. Additionally, the producers understood which topics were feasible or not as agenda points. They were also helpful when providing all the information the government needed to understand the problems they were facing. The high-value fruits sector had already communicated with the public sector to request solutions for some of their problems – especially the Ministry of Agriculture – so the NIPDB team knew they had a constructive agenda focused on sectoral issues.

Politically uncontroversial. The high-value fruits sector was away from the focus of media and was not controversial from a political standpoint. Had the NIPDB chosen a politically controversial sector like fishing – within the context of the fish rot scandal – the sector would have lacked the space to experiment and adapt that was essential for the pilot of PTF, and it would have been very difficult to identify and solve productivity constraints amid the media coverage.

3.3 Summary of Preliminary Work

The analysis of potential sectors was followed by internal meetings to decide based on the requirements' checklist. The next step was to conduct a series of interviews to provide a final check on the sector selection and set the basis to kick-start the task force. The team from NIPDB interviewed private and public sector players from relevant areas. These one-on-one interviews were focused on:

- *Check the expectations and bandwidth of potential participants.* The list of candidates to participate in the task force meetings shall include people with a constructive attitude who would be open and were able to prioritize the discussions on productivity, rather than demanding interventions to boost their profitability – in the case of the private sector – or develop political interests – in the case of the public sector. The interviews were meant to inform on the sector and to screen the right group of agents in the task force.
- *Come up with an initial list of constraints.* During the preliminary interviews, the NIPDB team inquired about the main constraints – as perceived by participants – to productivity in the sector. This provided an initial set of constraints to feed the discussions at the table during the first meetings. Additionally, the constraints were associated with potential solutions, providing inputs to start identifying agents of change from the public sector that could work on those solutions.
- *Have a clear perspective on the task force's goals.* In addition to the broad goals of increasing productivity and value-added, the task force needed

specific goals for the sector. These could be related to increasing exports, achieving market diversification, or enhancing competitiveness. Although the NIPDB and Harvard Growth Lab teams thought it was too early and there was not enough information to define a concrete set of goals, this was a requirement from the Government of Namibia when greenlighting the task force, and the preliminary interviews helped develop a narrative about potential goals and impacts.
- *Identify relevant participants and gauge their internal cohesion.* One key consideration when choosing private sector stakeholders for the task force meetings was that the selection of participants should not be biased or influenced by personal criteria. To the contrary, during the preliminary interviews, the NIPDB team continuously asked whether they should invite other players to the meetings. The team kept the door open during the first few meetings to ensure they achieved the highest level of sector representation in the task force.
- *Inputs for the task force's agenda.* The previous points – together with the background research done on each candidate sector during the selection period – were used to inform the first meeting's agenda, especially the list of constraints. The participants also expected to see their views expressed in the preliminary meetings in the task force agenda. The initial set of constraints were the most critical talking points. Aside from these, the initial meetings were also meant to cover potential policy solutions that the private sector had voiced before in the interview process.

All in all, once there was enough information to decide when and how to kickstart the PTF, the only step left was to convene the different participants. The important thing was to get started and start learning. The goal during the initial research stage and preliminary interviews was not to develop a comprehensive understanding of the sector, but to provide talking points to help the team start quickly and efficiently. Table 1 provides a summary of the set-up process for the Namibian high-value fruits PTF.

4 Running the Task Force: Identifying Problems and Advancing Solutions

The case of the high-value fruits in Namibia presents valuable learnings when it comes to running an efficient task force that leads to productivity gains. The challenges a task force of this nature faces are twofold: (1) How can we identify the most binding constraints to productivity? and (2) How can we solve them? Each of these questions was associated with multiple other challenges in terms of strategy (how to prioritize constraints?), research and mapping the policy space (what are the optimal policies to solve for a given constraint?), and

Table 1 Summary of the setup process of the Namibian productivity task force

Key Concepts	Guiding Principle	Namibia's Case
Decision-making Authority	The task force needs the power to mobilize different government entities across a range of policy areas.	The Harvard Growth Lab proposed productivity task forces to the Government of Namibia at cabinet level, which was well received.
Team Composition	The task force needs high-level political champions and a dedicated team within the chosen hosting entity.	Namibia's team included high-level government officials (political champions) and a dedicated team at NIPDB composed of a mix of senior, middle manage and junior officers.
Hosting Entity	The entity hosting and running the task force should have a high standing within government and convening capacity across public entities.	The Namibia Investment Promotion Board (NIPDB) for its technical capacity, convening capacity across government (located at the President's office), and its autonomous nature.
Administrative Capacity and Political Support	The task force team should strike the right balance between technical capacity and political participation and support.	The Namibian team had senior officials who understood politics (champions) and mid-level and junior officials with technical skills to identify policy reforms and coordinate with multiple stakeholders (policy officers).
Sector Analysis	The sectors should be chosen considering their growth potential, employment creation, and export capacity.	The high-value fruits sector in Namibia was chosen to pilot the task force, for its potential to deliver export-led growth, increasing global demand, and domestic factors such as underutilized land and a high unemployment in rural areas.

Table 1 (cont.)

Key Concepts	Guiding Principle	Namibia's Case
Checklist for Sector Selection	The sector should meet certain criteria: having enough players, some form of preexisting self-organization and cohesion, an agenda with impact potential, participants with a constructive attitude, and not being politically controversial.	The high-value fruits sector in Namibia met all these criteria. NIPDB proposed it after a thorough analysis of the available options and interviews with private sector stakeholders, and cabinet validated it.
Preliminary Work	The selection process should be followed by (i) internal meetings to evaluate which sector is the best fit, and (ii) a series of interviews to provide a final check and to provide priors to kick-start the task force.	The Namibian team followed this process, conducting internal meetings and interviews across private sector stakeholders within different candidate industries and various rounds of validation within government that resulted in the high-value fruits sector.

Source: Own elaboration

implementation (who shall be convened for an effective intervention and who will lead the reform process?). In this section, we delve into the specific constraints identified by the task force, the strategies proposed to address them, and the corresponding implementation issues (or the lack thereof).

As mentioned in the previous section, the team running the task force already had a preliminary list of constraints that resulted from previous research work and the interviews with private sector stakeholders in the sectors that preceded the launching of the initiative. This was crucial for informing the initial meetings and providing the initial sessions with a clear agenda. The preliminary work facilitated the identification of a concrete and actionable list of constraints in the very first meeting carried out in December 2021. The public sector got a sense of the most crucial problems and how to prioritize interventions right from the beginning. The task force team extended invitations to all the public institutions needed to address the preliminary list of constraints, guaranteeing the relevance of actors invited to sit at the table.

At the same time, the Harvard Growth Lab contributed to the discussion and the preparatory work with benchmark cases that informed the process, which started with a case study of nontraditional exports in Peru. Peru has been one of the most successful countries in exporting fruits and vegetables – particularly grapes and blueberries – and had the potential to deliver valuable insights to inform policy strategies aimed at increasing the sector's productivity and exports in Namibia. It is worth noting that some of the regions of Peru where high-value fruits like blueberries and table grapes boomed are also semi-desertic areas like the South of Namibia, where most of the high-value fruit farms are located. Likewise, the output of grapes and blueberries in Namibia at the time was also reminiscent of what was seen in Peru twenty years ago. The case study of Peru highlighted the following aspects that were deemed relevant to the Namibian experience:

Land property regulations enabled the expansion of agriculture. Although controversial for different reasons, the land reform of the early 1990s set the legal basis for the expansion of Peru's fruit and vegetable sector. The reform increased the limits on privately owned hectares of land, expropriated dry and idle land from the communal regions, and enabled investment in irrigation infrastructure. From 1997 to 2008, the government sold around 68,000 hectares in the coastal areas. The average size of land sold was 350 hectares, a hundred times larger than the size of the average property from the region, 3.5 hectares in 1997 (World Bank, 2017).

Fiscal incentives fostered private investment. The Law of Agriculture promotion from 2000 (27360) created a sort of "special economic zone" for agriculture through tax incentives. These tax incentives included accelerated depreciation of 20% of the annual investments in irrigation and water, a corporate tax rate of 15% (instead of the regular 30%), and the allowance to recover value-added taxes paid on capital goods up to five years after the corresponding investment.

The government played a crucial role in expanding the use of irrigation technologies. Public investment in irrigation systems grew at a compounded annual growth rate of over 16% from 2001 to 2015 (Ruiton Cabanillas et al., 2022). As a result, the percentage of arable land equipped for irrigation went from 49% in 2000–2002 to 75% in 2016–2018 (FAOSTAT). Lastly, the government pursued policies to guarantee access to drip irrigation techniques for both large and small farms.

The export boom coincided with a big push in trade policy. The government signed multiple free trade agreements, including treaties with Canada (2008), the United States (2009), and the European Union (2013). There was a big push in promoting the Peruvian brand abroad, with significant efforts on investment attraction and export promotion carried in coordination with private sector stakeholders.

Building a phytosanitary authority was a critical factor in the industry's success. Before the boom, there was no capable plant health authority in Peru. Still, the Peruvian agency – Servicio Nacional de Sanidad Agraria or SENASA – acquired the required skills and developed a modern organization that played a significant role in agreeing protocols to open markets and boost exports. International cooperation through the Inter-American Development Bank was an essential part of developing a capable plant health authority.

There are no one-size-fits-all solutions to the problem of achieving sustainable and inclusive economic growth. This also applied to the productivity task forces in Namibia, which had to work to find local solutions for local problems. Nevertheless, there were many parallels between the Peruvian and Namibian cases of high-value exports. Although it did not make sense to copy-paste the Peruvian strategy toward the sector, understanding how it worked provided valuable insights for the public and private stakeholders at the Namibian task force. These research inputs helped NIPDB prioritize topics and questions during the preliminary work. In the following sections, we describe the constraints the task force decided to focus on and the proposed solutions.

4.1 Market Access

In a small open economy like Namibia, growth can only be promoted by tapping into international demand. Thus, accessing international markets was a critical element of success. In turn, phytosanitary or plant health regulations are crucial to enable market access in industries like high-value fruits. Food and fruit imports have become increasingly regulated to secure health standards. Each country has its own set of phytosanitary rules and certifications that exporters need to comply with to access their market, and many of those can take years to obtain – becoming nontariff barriers to trade.

In addition to that, international standards started to be adopted in the early 1990s.[4] Exporters depend on their national phytosanitary authority to work with their counterparts in other countries, make applications, organize missions, and implement local regulations that meet international standards. The Peru case showcased the importance of SENASA's role in enabling exports to different markets. From the producers' perspective, market access was the only difference between Namibia and competitors like Peru.

In the first task force meeting, the producers described Namibia's plant health agency as more of a barrier to exports than an effective enabler. The plant health authority was having a negative impact on the development of the private sector because of several factors:

- The relationship between the agency and the producers was not constructive. Although they were meant to work together to increase production and health standards, they distrusted each other. The PTF was an opportunity to turn the page and start with a clean slate.
- The agency was underfunded, which resulted in poor service delivery. The state of public capabilities in the agency ultimately had a negative impact on the producers' capacity to access foreign markets. According to the farmers at the table, South Africa was close to cutting fruit imports from Namibia at different points in time during the 2000s because the plant health regulator did not file monitoring reports for fruit flies.

Ultimately, the agency became a barrier to gaining access to the most strategic market for table grapes: China. The process for implementing the plant health protocols required by China was at a standstill when the PTF started. The producers had exhausted all their resources to work with the agency on this issue. Access to the Chinese market was the most relevant growth opportunity for grape growers and where they needed to collaborate the most with the public sector. Although this was not the priority for other high-value fruit producers (for instance, dates, whose exports were directed mainly to Middle Eastern countries), it would work as a pilot experience for unlocking access to strategic international markets and providing further growth opportunities for all. It was

---

[4] The first International Standard for Phytosanitary Measures (ISPM) was adopted in 1993. See FAO, 2023a.

a matter of implementing requirements from China and negotiating the protocols. They believed that if they had a successful negotiation, they could gain a competitive advantage vis-à-vis other exporters like South Africa. The neighboring country had old protocols with China that required the produce to be frozen 72 hours before selling it in the market, so it was important for the Namibian authorities to aim at having protocols that did not include that clause.

However, the level of distrust between the producers and the plant health authorities at the Ministry of Agriculture, Water and Land Reform (MAWLR) was such that the latter questioned the producers' capacity to increase production if they effectively gained access to the Chinese market. The PTF meetings were helpful for the public counterpart to understand what accessing China meant for the private sector. At the time, Namibia's table grapes' annual production was equivalent to China's daily consumption. Unlocking the Chinese market would enable producers to grow by orders of magnitude while at the same time strengthening the industry's technical and productive capabilities in the long term.

Furthermore, African exports of fruits had been increasing for a decade. Figure 6 shows that Europe was one of the leading markets for African fruits: France, Germany, the Netherlands, the UK, and Spain comprised around 40% of

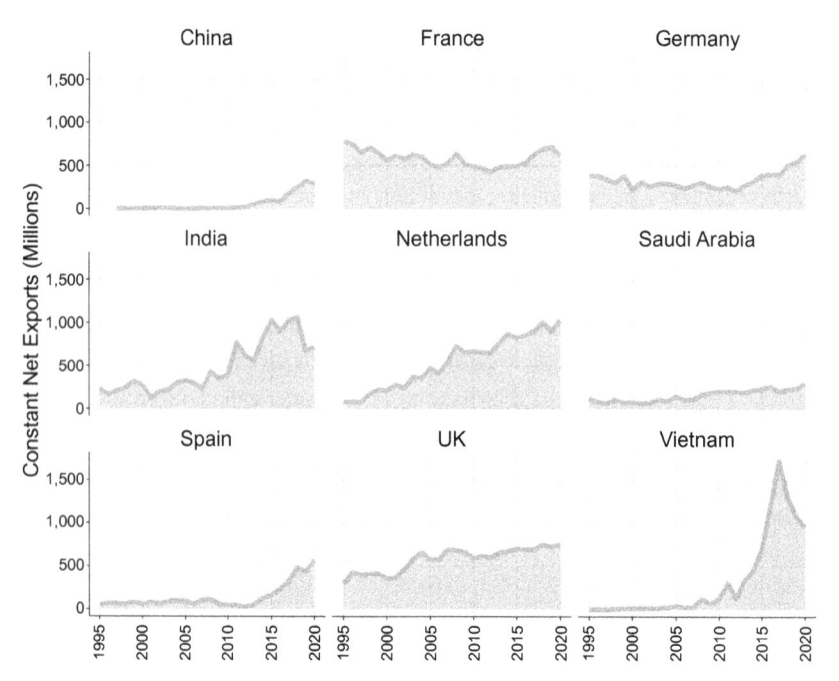

Figure 6 Export destinations of fruit and nuts from Africa (top 9)
Source: Atlas of Economic Complexity

fruit exports. The growth in African fruit exports to the Netherlands, led by South Africa (60%), was noteworthy and showed potential to increase and diversify exports from Southern Africa to the European markets – to which Namibia already had access. Figure 6 also shows that several Asian countries presented high-potential opportunities for Africa. China, India, and Vietnam had significantly increased fruit imports from Africa in the previous decade. The growing demand from these markets implied that accessing the Chinese market could be a game changer for the Namibian high-value fruits industry and a stepping stone to access other markets in Asia.

Exports to China were especially important because of the size and dynamics of the Chinese markets. Figure 7 shows that Egypt and South Africa were the main drivers of the African fruit export boom to China. South Africa is a relevant point of comparison for Namibia because of the shared history and multiple similarities. Conversely, Egypt's climate conditions are quite similar to those of Namibia. Other countries in Southern Africa, like Zimbabwe, managed to enter the Chinese fruit markets – which resulted in a 200% export growth between 2016 and 2020 (Figure 7). In all these cases, the plant health regulator was a critical factor in enabling access.[5]

During the first PTF meetings, the group agreed that there were two layers of the problem of plant health in Namibia: (a) in the short run, if the government did not prioritize plant health as a policy area, they were not going to gain access to the Chinese market for Namibian table grapes, and (b) in the long-run, they would not help the sector grow if they did not strengthen the capacity of the plant health regulator.

In the short run, the leading solution was to assign a high-level policy team in charge of the issue and use the PTF meetings as a communication channel to report progress. The presence of a high-level officer from MAWLR was vital in moving forward on this front. The MAWLR representative took charge of a process that was at a standstill: Negotiating and implementing the Chinese protocols. He had the administrative capacity and political authority to coordinate with other public agencies, such as the Namibian embassy in China. He took responsibility for the issue and used the meetings to report progress – which was well received by the producers. By February 2023, the Chinese authorities had provided feedback on Namibia's request. The analysis identified a series of pests that posed a significant risk for China. On the other hand, the

---

[5] A more recent case of relevance for Namibia was avocado exports from Kenya. The KEPHIS is a highly competent phytosanitary authority that has recently managed to gain access to the Chinese markets while dealing with serious issues like fruit fly infestations. For more information see: www.ntu.edu.sg/cas/news-events/news/details/fresh-kenyan-avocados-to-be-exported-to-china-soon and www.kephis.org/index.php/kenya-to-export-avocado-fruits-to-china.

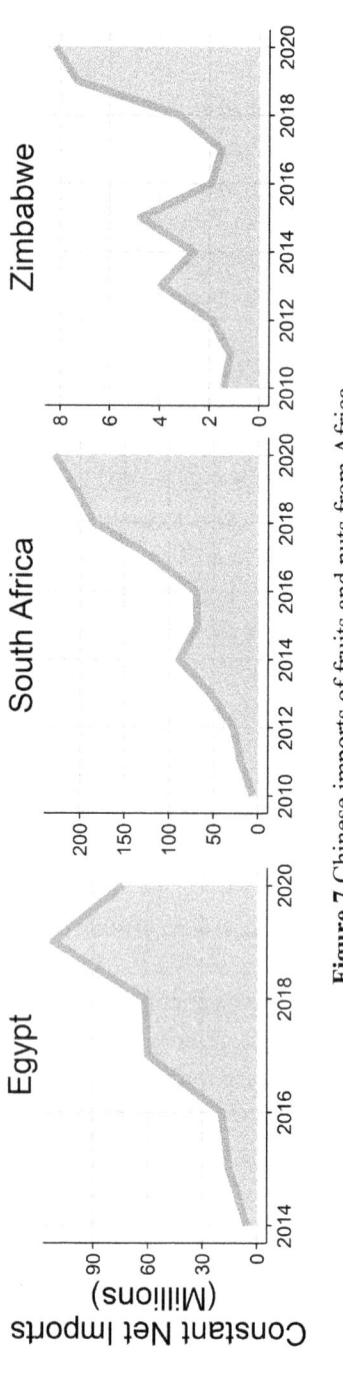

Figure 7 Chinese imports of fruits and nuts from Africa

Source: Atlas of Economic Complexity

Namibian counterparts conducted their own pest risk analysis in collaboration with the grape growers. They confirmed the occurrence of some of the pests identified by China but did not find evidence of others. Additionally, MAWLR authorities had already signed an umbrella agreement with China and were waiting for the signatures from their counterparts. The negotiation process, analyses, and implementation of plant health procedures were specific to grapes but worked as a template for other high-value fruits and agriculture products.

In the long run, MAWLR decided to call for applications to expand the technical team at the plant health regulator. This was a crucial step in acquiring the skills they needed to do a series of tasks necessary for unlocking growth in the sector – mainly regarding compliance with international standards, but also in assisting small and medium producers in improving their sanitary protocols. Doing this while reporting to the task force helped build trust between the private and the public sectors. The plant health division defined the skills they needed in collaboration with the private sector, and the private sector saw an opportunity to participate and actively collaborate in a process that would bring them benefits.

Other issues related to barriers to international market access that were mentioned in the PTF were:

- As mentioned in the previous section, the ports of Namibia were gaining comparative advantage vis-à-vis Cape Town. However, at the time, the concern was that Namibian ports were farther away from the farms than the port of Cape Town, so the farmers had been exporting their produce through the latter. They would have been interested in utilizing the port of Walvis Bay in Namibia. However, the problem was that neither the port nor the producers had the scale required by vessels to stop in Namibia. Additionally, administrative and logistical issues increased the cost of using both the ports of Lüderitz and Walvis Bay vis-a-vis Cape Town. As mentioned before, the problems with the Cape Town Port ended up raising their costs up to the point where producers were urged to develop the Walvis Bay route to remain competitive.
- Paperwork represented a hurdle for exporters, often done in situ in the border posts, resulting in extensive delays. The process needed to be modernized and digitized. This was not a significant issue affecting market access, but it imposed higher costs on the producers.

4.2 Access to Seeds and Plant Variety Protection

In addition to market access, key inputs like seeds were another essential ingredient for the competitiveness of the high-value fruits sector. In today's agriculture, that means access to modified or improved seeds. Developing seeds and plant

Box 2 Research inputs for developing a plant health regulator

Following the first task force meeting, the participants expressed interest in learning more about how plant health regulation evolved in Peru. In response to that request, the Harvard Growth Lab did a deep dive into the process of building a plant health regulator in Peru. This was meant to provide policy and research inputs to the task force and help frame the discussion with relevant points of comparison between Namibia and Peru. The following are the main takeaways regarding the development of SENASA:

- *The plant health authority had political and administrative independence*. This allowed them to build administrative capacity in the long run by avoiding changing leadership due to political volatility. It also helped SENASA resist political pressure to protect certain crops or sectors. This is a common theme among plant health regulators worldwide; they sometimes impose nontariff barriers to protect domestic production.
- *SENASA's Human Capital was crucial for its development*. From top to bottom, the agency's decision-making instances were populated with people with technical expertise and policy capacity. The agency also managed to have a flexible enough structure to learn by working with the private sector –although the staff was mostly public policy experts and did not necessarily have experience in the sector. Another salient feature of the strategy was to build regional state capacity: Being close to farmers kept the agency close to producers and their most relevant issues while at the same time avoiding the problems stemming from excessive centralization.
- *Up-front public investments in state capacity*. To start up the agency, a significant public investment was required for assembling a technical team, making capital investments in regional offices, acquire laboratory equipment, and launching national campaigns. Once settled as an effective plant health regulator, SENASA earned over 50% of its budget through service fees.
- *The agency was effective in engaging with the private sector*. SENASA was able to strike the right balance between supporting the private sector through services and enabling their access to international markets and overseeing the companies to ensure they abide by regulations. Additionally, an effective engagement helped the public officers learn what they needed from the private sector to be able to draft laws and regulations. Yet because the private sector was included during the

> Box 2 (cont.)
>
> process of drafting and discussion of regulations, they were aware of their obligations and why they were in the sector's long-term interest.
>
> - *International cooperation was essential to develop state capacity.* The Inter-American Development Bank (IDB) played a key role in accelerating the development of SENASA in Peru through technical cooperation programs, as they facilitated access to knowhow and skills from foreign experts.

varieties is a complex process that requires investment in research and development (R&D), and plant breeders[6] hold intellectual property rights on their varieties. In the absence of regulations, the international trade of plant varieties would threaten the returns of plant breeders and discourage R&D. To ensure plant breeders' rights at the international level, a group of countries adopted the International Convention for the Protection of New Varieties of Plants in 1961. The convention and its implementation are administered by the International Union for the Protection of New Varieties of Plants (UPOV).[7]

Namibia's approach toward securing access and safeguarding plant varieties had predominantly depended on initiatives at the regional level, which had not produced the expected results. This approach included efforts such as the African Regional Intellectual Property Organization's (ARIPO) bid to join UPOV (initiated in 2009), the establishment of the Arusha Protocol in 2015 (introducing a regional mechanism for the protection of plant varieties offering a unified legal framework with consistent and explicit principles for its member states), and the development of the Protocol for Protection of New Varieties of Plants in collaboration with eight countries from the Southern African Development Community (SADC) (Fortunato & Enciso-Valdivia, 2023).

However, at the time of the launch of the PTF, Namibia was not part of UPOV, and the farmers faced difficulties accessing international cultivars. Less than 5% of farmers in commercial and communal land areas used improved seeds, and only one of twenty-two regional seed companies (and no global companies) were present in Namibia. The participants in the high-value fruits task force identified this as a critical constraint. They voiced their need to access high-yield and state-of-the-art seed varieties to compete in international markets. It was not only

---

[6] These are for the most part biotech firms, but there are also public institutions and smaller firms developing plant varieties across the globe.

[7] The convention has been revised several times since its adoption. By 2023, there were seventy-eight countries that were members of UPOV and nineteen others had initiated the process of joining.

a matter of productivity, but often, it was also a matter of product quality. Some markets demand specific types of crops or produce that require specific seeds. Namibia was not only absent from UPOV but did not have a bill that regulated and protected plant breeders' rights. This limited the farmers' ability to import varieties from international companies, which required a legal framework to ensure the recognition of their intellectual property rights.

In 2018, Namibia sanctioned the Seed and Seed Varieties Act, which regulated the registry and certification of seeds in Namibia. Nonetheless, there was still a legal gap in protecting plan breeders' rights. The Plant Breeders and Farmers' Rights Bill remained a draft in discussion since 2009. As the public sector officials made clear in the PTF, the government seemed reticent to enact a plant variety protection system mainly because of its potentially harmful effect on small farmers. This concern was based on two ideas: (a) the farmers' rights to access food could be in contradiction with the breeders' rights if the former had to pay royalties for the use of seeds; (b) both the country's sovereignty over its biodiversity and the local traditional knowledge could be threatened by the recognition of international companies' rights over varieties that might be Indigenous to Namibia.

To solve this critical constraint without hurting small farmers, the task force produced a series of research inputs to help define a path forward. The output was expected to create common ground across stakeholders to accept that becoming a member of UPOV was not in direct contradiction with protecting small farmers' rights and safeguarding both biodiversity and local traditional knowledge. The main insights from that effort were:

- If Namibia decided to enact a plant variety protection system and join UPOV, the country would also benefit from designing a set of complementary policies to conserve national genetic resources for the use of local farmers and protect farmers' rights. Kenya, for example, had developed a system in which the protection of domestically bred varieties was a responsibility of public institutions, which facilitated access to new plants for domestic small farmers under privileged conditions (Kimani, 2018). Additionally, the UPOV framework already allowed for exemptions in specific cases, such as using varieties for subsistence farming or noncommercial purposes would be one of them.
- The patenting of cultivars covered a subset of commercial varieties, out of which horticultural products were the most protected (70%), followed by extensive crops like maize or wheat (15%), but did not necessarily include several of the varieties that were used in subsistence or small-scale agriculture (Fortunato & Enciso-Valdivia, 2023).
- The small-scale and subsistence farmers were already producing for domestic markets and self-consumption without needing improved seeds; a plant

varieties protection system would not necessarily introduce hurdles to their current production practices. Additionally, it was likely that many of them remained informal as Namibia joined UPOV.
- There was a possibility that implementing a plant variety protection system would have brought positive spillovers for small-scale farmers, as they could access improved seeds that brought more resiliency to climate hardships and higher yields.
- To promote local innovation in plant varieties, the legal framework would have had to be accompanied by public policies and institutions that advanced biotechnology and crop science research. These institutions would work closely with local farmers to provide improved locally developed or imported seeds.[8]

These findings helped the task force's private and public stakeholders agree on a plan for Namibia to join UPOV. The officers from MAWLR restarted the dialog with UPOV authorities to get their feedback on the draft of the Plant Breeders and Farmers' Rights Bill. Again, the task force worked as a communication channel that benefited the private and public sectors in acquiring valuable information for planning. As far as we know, Namibia initiated the procedure of acceding to the UPOV convention in February 2024, although the prospects of an official ascension are uncertain because of reasons we explain in Section 5.1.[9]

4.3 Access to Knowhow and Issues at the Border Control Posts

As an export-oriented activity, producing high-value fruits requires frequent interaction with international agents from different fields. Producers not only engage with buyers from other countries but also with foreign consultants or experts they hire to ensure compliance with international standards. In the case of Namibia, the primary source for both (buyers and experts) is South Africa. South Africa has a competitive agriculture sector – especially in the fruits industry – and is also an attractive market for Namibia in terms of size and proximity. To access the knowledge and expertise required to conquer that opportunity, Namibian producers needed a mechanism to ease the entry of high-skilled immigrants.

Namibia's regulations for cross-border transit included collecting VAT on foreign vehicles crossing its borders inward. Although individuals could request an exemption or a tax rebate, the process was burdensome, according to the producers in the task force. They would try to bring a foreign buyer or expert by

---

[8] The Government of Namibia's current approach to plant variety development has been focused on food security, and has not prioritized varieties for commercial use, especially those that are export-oriented.

[9] See www.upov.int/export/sites/upov/members/en/pdf/status.pdf. Consulted in June 2024.

car through the border – even for a two-day meeting – only to find that the person would be retained, paying a tax on their vehicle, and going through time-consuming paperwork. Another possibility would have been to bring foreign knowhow as Namibian residents on a permanent basis, but the process to obtain work visas for highly skilled foreigners was very restrictive and subject to many regulatory hurdles. The stated reason among government officials and politicians alike was that unemployment were already high among young graduates from Namibian universities, and allowing foreign workers into the country would only aggravate it. They tended to perceive foreigners as substitutes, when in fact having the right knowhow available would have probably allowed for the creation of new jobs for Namibians.

4.4 Access to Water

Namibia's water resources are scarce as it is the most arid country in sub-Saharan Africa. Climate and natural conditions make it challenging for agriculture to thrive. Nonetheless, agricultural activity happens where water is available, even if at a higher cost to farmers. As mentioned earlier, the high-value fruits farmers are located primarily in southern Namibia, where the Orange River represents the most important source of water. In 2013, the Government of Namibia started to work on the project of the *Neckartal Dam* (a project dating back to German colonial times), which became the most significant water storage facility in Namibia once completed in 2019. The dam was installed in the Fish River, an affluent of the Orange River.

Exploiting water resources from the Orange River basin was a topic of discussion between Namibia and South Africa because the latter was also reliant on water downstream that basin and its capacity would be negatively affected. To unlock the potential of agriculture in southern Namibia, the country had to develop irrigation and water management infrastructure to make the best use of the basin. That involved a negotiation process with South Africa to ensure that easing water access for Namibian farmers upstream the Orange River would not have counterproductive impacts in the neighboring country. The PTF became a communication channel between the government and the farmers about these issues, thus helping move forward and creating awareness of the negotiation process.

4.5 Land Tenure

The northern regions of Namibia have comparatively better conditions for agriculture, but because of the communal land tenure system, there is no market for acquiring or leasing land. The allocation of land is decided by the local and regional authorities, and these are often reticent to work with foreign private sector investors. Additionally, the northern municipalities' balance sheets depend on the income derived from auctioning the land, distorting prices and distribution. The inflow of agriculture capital to northern Namibia faces the challenge of dealing with the particularities of the land tenure system.

Moreover, the Agricultural Land Act (1995) required that to use the tenure of communal land as collateral for applying for bank loans, the person applying for the credit needed approval from MAWLR. This requirement resulted in bureaucratic hurdles and made it virtually impossible to access credit by using land leases as collaterals in the North. Furthermore, this resulted in barriers to access and credit shortages for small communal farmers looking into acquiring capital to increase productivity. While commercial farmers often secured loans using their land or houses, communal farmers were more inclined to depend on their livestock, third-party support, and other assets as collateral for loan applications (Fortunato & Enciso-Valdivia, 2023).

Before the PTF started, the government was aware of the challenges that the land tenure system presented for developing productive agriculture in northern Namibia. Once again, the task force was instrumental as an information revealing mechanism, whereby government got valuable insights from potential investors interested in developing farms in the north. This was especially relevant in the decision to lease portions of state-owned land to the private sector. In 2008, the government started a Green Schemes Policy aimed at developing irrigation infrastructure in the northern regions of Namibia. These irrigation projects also included extensive portions of land that the government administered through AgriBusDev, a state-owned enterprise dedicated to agriculture.[10] More than a decade later, the projects had not managed to become profitable; but rather represented a significant burden for the Namibian public budget and scarce resources were vastly underutilized. This policy failure led the government to abandon the idea that a state-owned enterprise had to lead agricultural development in northern Namibia and opened the way for a policy strategy where the private sector had a pivotal role in developing commercial farms.

4.6 Other Constraints

Often in PPDs, the private sector puts the emphasis on the importance of government subsidies or other types of market interventions to compensate for the lack of competitiveness resulting from other constraints – which they perceive as harder to tackle.

In Namibia's high-value fruits task force, one of the top-of-mind factors impacting the cost of production was perceived to be electricity. According to

---

[10] See www.agribusdev.org.na/ for more information.

producers in the PTF, the share of electricity in total production cost was too high. That was a reasonable hypothesis, considering that Namibia imported over 80% of its electricity from South Africa, which had been experiencing a major electricity crisis for some time. However, neither South Africa's nor Namibia's electricity prices were significantly high when compared to the rest of the world (Hausmann et al., 2022). Additionally, the outages that severely affected South African businesses were not an issue in Namibia, as South African electricity authorities had decided to safeguard electricity exports to Namibia – which were small when contrasted with domestic demand in South Africa.

Regarding taxes and subsidies, the private sector expressed concern that the Namibian Agronomic Board charged a fee for conducting farm food and health inspections. The phytosanitary certificates that resulted from these inspections were required for export, so in the view of the farmers these fees effectively worked as a tax on exports. However, this was a common practice globally. Plant health authorities usually finance themselves through the services they provide.

5 In Hindsight: Assessing the Impact of the High-Value Fruits PTF

It is challenging to evaluate the success of PPDs by means of strict indicators such as investment, employment, exports, or production. It is difficult to design a feasible identification strategy to establish causal inference in this type of multidimensional context where several policy interventions are occurring at the same time. To overcome these challenges and get a relative sense of the accomplishments and pitfalls of productivity task forces, we put our focus on three broad areas. First, we look at changes in the broad policy framework and government approach to the sector and to specific reforms on areas that were identified by the task force as barriers or constraints to productivity and competitiveness. Second, we look at specific indicators of the sector's economic performance, such as investments announced and executed, harvested area, and exports. And, third, we carried a series of interviews with the private sector stakeholders that have been participating in the task force for two and a half years, to gather a more qualitative assessment of the relative success or failure of the initiative.

5.1 Impacts on Government Approach to the Sector and Policy Reforms

The PTF helped build state capacity across government. The exercise of defining specific, actionable problems, brainstorming on potential solutions, and working together on implementation was critical for coordinating and strengthening different public entities that were disconnected from real-world problems of the high-value fruits sector. Paradoxically, these were agencies with decision-making power over critical issues – such as the plant health authority – but did not have any mechanism or direct channel to interact with private sector representatives, identify, and understand their most important hurdles to be competitive. In particular, the MAWLR greatly benefited from improved communication with private sector representatives.

The high-value fruits task force also had broader impacts on the government's overall narrative and strategy toward the agricultural sector in Namibia. At a time when the government was rethinking its state-led economic development model, the task force facilitated a shift of focus from central planning to providing incentives to enable and expand private sector involvement in agriculture. Previously, the government had assigned a pivotal role in its economic development strategy to state-owned enterprises (SOEs). In agriculture, AgriBusDev was the SOE in charge of the green schemes and public irrigation projects aimed at increasing output and employment. It was an effort to replicate the market mechanism by means of central planning, whereby government provided fertile land and inputs to small farmers, established prices for their produce, agglomerated their output on a public distributor, and imposed the sale of volume and prices toward public entities such as schools and hospitals. As it tends to happen, the exhaustion of public funds eased by the end of the super commodity price cycle had exposed all the drawbacks of the structure, their large fiscal cost, and low contribution to overall output. After several years of policy failures, the government decided to open the green schemes for private sector participation through a system of public bids that was informed by the inputs gathered at the PTF.

The PTF's impact extended significantly to Namibia's investment promotion landscape, fostering a more collaborative and solution-oriented approach among public institutions. The Namibia Investment Promotion and Development Board (NIPDB) leveraged the task force to develop trust and improve its coordination with public and private stakeholders. This facilitated the promotion of Namibia as an open and market-oriented economy, attracting foreign investment and boosting investor confidence. The PTF was showcased as an effort to foster public-private partnerships to highlight Namibia's commitment to creating a more conducive business environment.

Another signal of success of PTF – at least from the government's point of view – was NIPDB's decision to expand the initiative to two additional sectors. First, there was the launch of the PTF for the meat sector in 2022. The industry of bovine animals and derivates (processed, fresh, and frozen meat) was a relatively well-established business in Namibia. The sector was export-oriented; the producers had recently managed to access the US market, and there was strong unsatisfied demand coming from South Africa. Although the economic potential was undeniable, the industry faced several bottlenecks. First, the veterinary cordon fence – also known as the "red line" – prevented cattle ranching on the northern side from exporting because of the foot-and-mouth disease estimated to be prevalent on that area. This was a significant issue because most cattle in Namibia were north of the red line. Second, the prevalence of droughts severely damaged the sector's ability to develop higher-productivity practices. The main reason was that they had no financial or insurance instruments to hedge or recover from droughts (by developing alternative technologies for animal feed). Lastly, the productivity of most farms was relatively low because they lacked technology to help them increase cattle density and production.

The third task force was launched in 2023 for the film and television industry. It came to be called in the NIPDB the "new sector task force" (NSTF) because – different from high-value fruits and meat – the industry was relatively small in Namibia and did not have established companies that could potentially inform on the most important constraints. It was a rare experiment of launching a task force to learn from private sector stakeholders that have not decided to take upon large investments in Namibia but were rather located elsewhere. There were scattered efforts to produce content, and Namibia had been a location site for international movies such as "Mad Max: Fury Road," but there was no consistent production of audiovisual content. The NIPDB team invited a series of key players involved in the sector in neighboring country – particularly South Africa – and started developing a plan to inform on the most important constraints, promote the scenic Namibian locations, and attract foreign investment. At the time of writing these efforts were relatively incipient and consequently their influence and impacts are yet to be determined.

Regarding specific constraints discussed at the film and television task force, the only tangible improvement broadly recognized by all producers came in the access to foreign talent. The interactions and the relationship developed at the monthly meetings led the NIPDB to establish a dedicated official responsible from taking the visa requests from producers and securing its processing by the Ministry of Home Affairs and Immigration. The process allowed producers to hire foreign talent as well as to bring consultants from South Africa on two-year work permits, which eased the restriction on talent and increased the knowhow and efficiency of the sector. Access to foreign talent did not come at the expense of jobs for Namibians but rather helped to increase investments and create jobs that would not have been available otherwise. In practice, foreign talent in the high-value fruits sector was complementary to Namibians, not a substitute of local talent.

Coming back to the assessment of the government's role in the high-value fruits PTF, the main takeaway is that there was no significant progress in solving several of the main constraints as of August 2024. The issues have been discussed, well diagnosed, and in most cases, there were specific government actions outlined and even undertaken to alleviate or solve them. However, the thread had been lost somewhere along the way, due to a mixture of lack of follow-up or political willingness, or the classical lethargy of diplomatic channels.

Regarding Namibian membership in UPOV, no definitive progress was achieved. The MAWLR did start a dialog with UPOV authorities to get their feedback on the draft of the Plant Breeders and Farmers' Rights Bill but did not follow up on the recommendations. According to the producers at the task force, there was a long process of public consultation throughout 2022 and half of 2023 with small farmers, communities, and stakeholders, about the specific provisions of the legislative changes that needed to be enacted for Namibia to become a member of UPOV. That lengthy round of consultations probably reinforced the concerns of the MAWLR regarding the impact of UPOV provisions on small farmers, and the uncertainty surrounding the impacts of joining in case Namibia becomes a seed producer or takes advantage of indigenous plant varieties. The issue remained in the agenda from the inception of the PTF in December 2021 until August 2023. From then onward, there were no further updates or progress reported and the issue dropped from the discussion.

At the time of writing, no progress has been recorded either regarding access to the Chinese market. As a result of the discussions at the PTF, the Government of Namibia worked on all the necessary requests through diplomatic channels and initiated the protocols required. Chinese authorities had developed a particular protocol with South Africa – different from the one Namibia had signed with the European Union and the United Kingdom, where most of the Namibian exports of grapes and berries go – and demanded similar requirements from Namibia.

Some producers at the task force explained that China had identified six pests that needed to be monitored, which are included neither in European nor in UK protocols. For these six pests they demand a period of monitoring and reporting going from six to twelve months. According to them, the Namibian government does not have the equipment or the scientists required to analyze the pests and comply with the process. Private sector stakeholders even offered to buy the equipment in exchange for Namibia hiring the necessary talent at the plant health regulator, but the proposal did not move forward (to the extent of our knowledge). Others argued that the diplomatic process required to open the

Chinese market was extremely lengthy and cumbersome, and it was hard to track the exact status of the request across the different administrative levels on both governments. The NIPDB did not have the capacity to monitor progress across the different public entities involved – let alone across the Chinese ones. Whatever the reasons, the fact remains that no definitive progress had been made on access to the Chinese market at the time of writing and that probably led the grape farmers to abandon the PTF toward the end of 2023.

5.2 Impacts on Specific Indicators of Economic Performance in the Sector

The high-value fruits sector in Namibia recorded significant growth both before and after the inception of the PTF in December 2021. Figure 8 illustrates this trend through the harvested area of grape and date farms (left) and gross exports of grapes (right). Between 2018 and 2022, grape farms registered an increase of two thousand hectares or 28% in harvested area. In addition to that, grape farms had a robust export performance: Gross exports increased by 40% between 2020 and 2022. Similarly, the harvested area for dates – although at a much lower scale – more than tripled between 2017 and 2022. The expansion indicates a substantial investment in date farming, driven by growing demand and favorable market conditions. These trends in both harvested areas and export volumes underscore the dynamic nature of Namibia's high-value fruits sector. The expansion of harvested areas suggests that farmers are optimistic about prospects for the industry in Namibia, respond to market signals and have invested in increasing production capacity to meet rising demand.

It is still too early to attempt a formal policy evaluation of the PTF that could help pin down the specific economic impacts on the high-value fruits industry in Namibia. However, the sector's upward trend continued after the PTF stated, as seen in Figure 8 (right). In 2023, gross exports of grapes increased by 21% versus the previous year. This is not an outcome of the PTF. All we can say is that the initiative worked on issues in a sector that was already growing and continued growing during the PTF.

Two large investment announcements in the sector were made in 2023. First, two high-value fruit farms were among the four top fastest-growing companies in Namibia, according to Africa's Fastest Growing Companies Report 2023 (Financial Times & Statista, 2023). Due to outstanding profitability, these companies were investing in expanding their farms during 2023 (Amukeshe, 2023). Second, a company focused on the production of blueberries (Namibia Berries) announced a US$80 million investment over seven years to establish a 250-hectare farm in the Kavango East region under the communal land

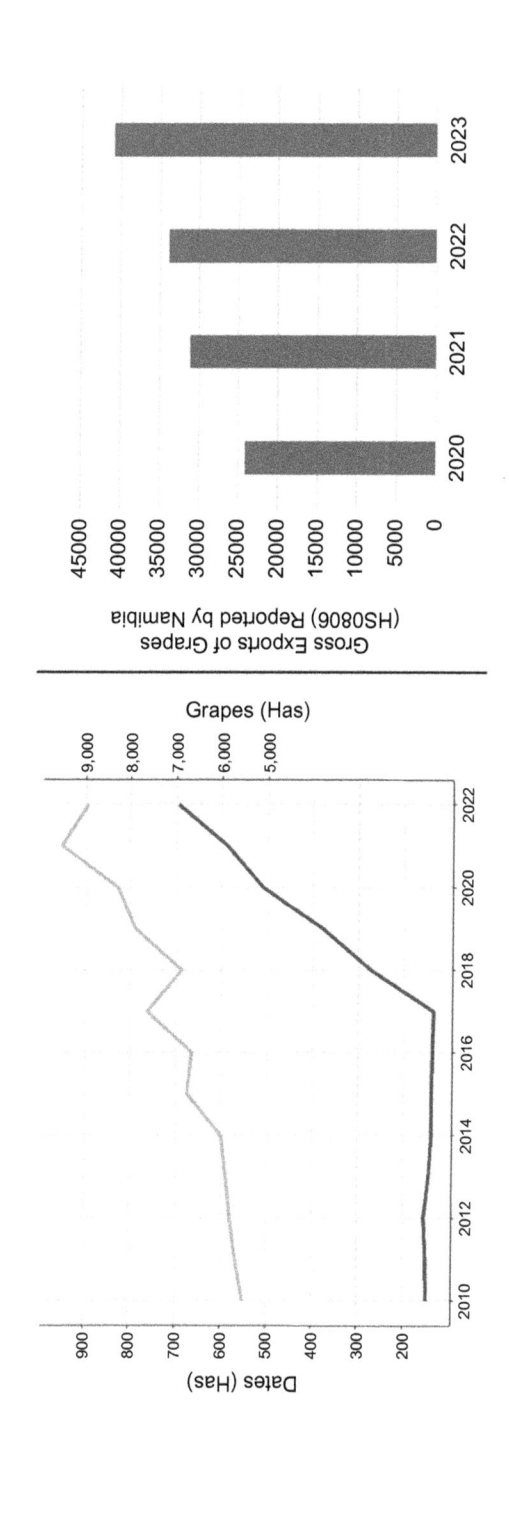

Figure 8 Harvested area of grapes and dates in 2010–2022 (left) and exports of grapes in 2020–2023 (right)

Sources: Harvested area from FAOSTAT and exports from UN COMTRADE

system. The project aimed to employ 800 staff and create around 7,000 jobs during harvest season, with the potential of having a large and significant impact on a region characterized by very low employment-to-population ratio and poverty. The two main investors are two large Spanish agri-food companies. The project was expected to export its first harvest in September 2024 (Food Business Africa, 2023).

The development of greenfield investments in the high-value fruits sector during 2023 cannot be attributed to the existence of the PTF. However, it does reflect improved relationships with government officials and a more friendly business environment, to which the PTF likely contributed. The PTF's focus on export-oriented facilitation through identifying and addressing the constraints identified previously has created good conditions for farmers to continue increasing their exports. Although the sector was already on a rising trend when the PTF was launched, coordination efforts to help the sector grow and the overall government openness towards private sector development created momentum that may have contributed to the continued increase of the sector's market valuation.

5.3 In Hindsight: Reflections from Private Sector Stakeholders in the PTF

Two and a half years after the inception of the high-value fruits PTF, we went back to interview a group of producers who had participated or continued participating in the meetings. The PTF met monthly for two full years (2022 and 2023), and by the beginning of 2024 had started to meet every two months. As mentioned earlier, grape farmers had decided to abandon the meetings as they perceived no progress beyond working visas for high-skill workers.

There is broad consensus that the launch of the policy initiative started off well, with high senior officials signaling their willingness to improve business conditions in the sector and most relevant agencies represented at the table. The initiative was met with a lot of enthusiasm from a group of farmers that did not have a forum to regularly meet government officials with decision making power over policy areas that were crucial to the sector. "We thought and everyone thought: This is going to move forward, they are willing to make an effort, and we are going play our part, not only to improve our business but also to make Namibia better."

Policy issues were discussed and identified, and the NIPDB fed the discussions with empirical evidence to support the identification of a set of actionable and relevant constraints. Throughout the meetings, issues were heard, discussed, and understood, but from then onwards – except for work permits for foreign talent – the government was unable to make progress. "When it came to actions to be taken, we seemed to have lost our way, issues fell on a limbo, there were too many government agencies involved in their resolution and did not always coordinated actions or even talked among them." The fact remains that it is hard to make progress if public–public coordination – coordination across agencies and sometimes between different levels of the public administration: national, federal, municipal – is not working well.

One factor contributing to the slowdown and loss of momentum of the PTF seems to be the lack of continuity of key government representatives at the task force. The Minister of Finance and Public Enterprises, Iipumbu Shiimi, chaired the meetings for a little more than a year – from launching in December 2021 until the beginning of 2023 – but then stopped attending. Margaret Matengu, Deputy Director and Head of Plant Health at the ministry, passed away in December 2023. According to various private sector stakeholders, Mrs. Matengu had both the will and the contacts within the administration necessary to push forward the process of opening the Chinese market. The transition to a new official was slow and did not leverage on the progress made and the knowhow that had been accumulated and the whole process faded away. Another high-level official at the MAWLR, Director General Penda Ithindi, attended the task force meetings throughout most of 2022 but in 2023 was reassigned to the Minister of Finance and replaced by a lower-ranking official. The withdrawal of high-level public officials caused the initiative to lose traction: "Task forces are very valuable as a communication channel, and as a tool to identify problems, but they don't have the teeth or political authorization to make things work anymore."

Given the lack of progress, it seems odd that the high-value fruits PTF continues to meet two and a half years later – even if at a lower frequency. Part of the reason seems to be that in a country coming out of apartheid where a significant degree of distrust remains between white farmers and black government officials, there are not many instances where these parties meet and have a chance to discuss issues of mutual interest. "An instance of interaction with government is still very valuable, even if the problems brought up are not sorted or dealt with: This is the only instance where we meet." The task force meetings have filled a vacuum, providing a space that participants consider valuable even in the absence of tangible and effective solutions. There seems to be an easing in preexisting distrust, as most producers at the task force recognize the willingness and honesty of the public servants they have interacted with.

Why keep on coming to these meetings? The truth is, we keep on coming because we love Namibia, and we need to help to promote change. We keep on coming because we are interacting with honest, reasonable people, trying their best to help. They are not just well organized. We want to help our country and will come to the meetings as many times as they call us.

6 A Roadmap for Productivity Task Forces: Reflections from Namibia

The Namibia case offers insightful lessons for devising a methodology to launch PPDs at the sector level – call it *Mesas Ejecutivas* (Peru) or Productivity Task Forces (Namibia). The process will differ across countries due to various factors such as cultural characteristics, state capacity, and politics. However, certain elements are crucial. This section reflects on these elements as part of the lessons learned from Namibia. Although the goal is for these reflections to be useful for other contexts, they are biased by the Namibian experience. These insights also attempt to synthesize ideas from the existing literature on the topic, which is rich and includes a wide range of experiences.

Section 3 presented practical considerations for establishing a high-value fruit PTF in Namibia. In this section, we shift our focus from operational aspects to reflections on pinpointing problems and solutions in Namibia. While the issues requiring industrial policy intervention can vary across countries and industries, they should have specific characteristics. In this section, we reflect on these characteristics based on the Namibian experience. For instance, focusing on unsolvable problems or identifying problems that come from inaccurate assessments could result in inefficient use of resources. Identifying a set of policies is a critical step in creating a successful task force. While context-specific factors influence policies, there should be general benchmarks for suitable policy formulation. For instance, if a task force concentrates on overly ambitious and long-term master plans, the policies may not yield effective results in the short term. This could lead to the task force's exhaustion and diminished effectiveness. We will call the task force's policies "productive development policies" following Crespi et al. (2014).

6.1 How to Identify Productivity Constraints?

Developing an effective process for problem identification is essential. Evidence shows that problem identification is crucial to "effective state capability building" (Andrews, 2013; Andrews et al., 2017). Identifying specific, relevant, and impactful problems in the context of productivity task forces is far from straightforward but is the first step forward. Often, policymakers try to come up with solutions without adequately considering the specific problems they have in front of them. The following is a set of criteria to help identify problems practically and productively. This is not an exhaustive or conclusive set; further iterations should help refine it.

6.1.1 Constraints Should Be as Binding as Possible

The primary attribute of productivity constraints is their ability to guide the task force in prioritizing interventions. An accurate evaluation of the sector's challenges paves the way for effective policy formulation and execution. In that sense, drawing concepts from the growth diagnostics toolkit (Hausmann et al., 2008) was helpful in the Namibia case. Although this methodology was initially designed to tackle national-level economic growth issues, several of its principles can be applied at the industry level.

If industry-specific constraints such as skills shortages, market access, or infrastructure issues were all equally binding, stakeholders would need to find ways to address them to make tangible progress. However, that is rarely the case. Some constraints will be more binding or have a more significant negative impact on overall growth. The primary task of a productivity task force is to identify those issues that appear to be binding constraints on productivity and deliver adequate solutions.

6.1.2 Productivity versus Profitability

When evaluating whether the task force is working on the correct problems, a critical dimension is whether these are productivity oriented. Naturally, firms aim to boost their profits by expanding their margins or creating new ventures. In private-public dialogs, the private sector is expected to seek ways to enhance profitability directly and without productivity gains, often by requesting government assistance to reduce costs (via subsidies or tax breaks) or protect them from imports (a mechanism to enable them to exist while remaining uncompetitive). If the government concentrates on profitability-oriented policies like subsidies or trade protection, these interventions compensate for the firms' low productivity instead of boosting it. In that case, public policy results in profitability gains without productivity improvements, which is what we refer to in the dichotomy "Productivity Vs. Profitability". These two concepts are not necessarily contradictory. Firms will definitely become more profitable if the government helps solve productivity problems in their sector or if they manage to unlock access to international markets. The critical point that we make here is that a productivity task force should focus on productivity problems rather than increasing profitability directly via direct market interventions.

What does increasing productivity look like? Multiple factors can constrain productivity at the sector level. These vary across countries and, sometimes, across regions within countries. They negatively impact firms' operational and business capacity within an industry. These could be infrastructure issues like high electricity prices or frequent outages, difficulties accessing high-skilled labor, lack of access to finance, or regulatory burdens that increase operational costs. The main characteristic to consider is that they are problems that explain why productivity is low in an industry or, at least, lower than expected – which prevents exports from growing, investments to come, or jobs from being created. Regarding the high-value fruits PTF in Namibia, issues with market access, plant health regulator, or border controls were more related to the efficient provision of public goods that their competitors likely enjoy in their countries.

As mentioned before, it is usually the case that private sector representatives will perceive that they need government support in the form of transfers or tariff protection instead of inputs that enhance their competitiveness. The Namibian Agronomic Board commissioned an agricultural survey of the fruit sector, and they found that over 70% of producers were not implementing any food safety systems in their farms, but most of them expressed their hope for more government "protection to boost local fruit production" (Namibian Agronomic Board, 2023: 6).

6.1.3 Supply-Side or Demand-Side Issues

Another relevant dimension for identifying productivity constraints is whether these are supply- or demand-side issues. This categorization does not necessarily help distinguish good versus bad problems because productivity problems can be both supply- or demand-driven. Instead, it is an additional relevant layer to take into account when analyzing the type of problems a sector faces. Problems in the supply of goods or services are often easier to identify because they affect firms' productivity through the production process, like the lack of appropriate infrastructure or the scarcity of inputs. Nevertheless, a task force can also target demand-side problems. As mentioned before, one of the binding constraints that Namibia's high-value fruits task force decided to work on was a demand-side issue: market access. Market access also affects an industry's productivity through scalability. Enabling market access is productivity-enhancing because it forces industries to comply with standards, increase scale, and adopt technology.

6.1.4 Problem Deconstruction

A problem should be decomposed into practical questions and actionable items to make it manageable (Andrews et al., 2017). The ideas presented in this section aim to be guidelines for problem deconstruction. It is crucial that the task force thinks about problems that are as binding as possible, that are productivity-oriented, of either supply or demand. However, other considerations are essential for identifying manageable problems. Andrews et al. (2017) provide a comprehensive toolkit for this type of endeavor. The Problem-Driven Iterative Approach (PDIA) they developed relies heavily on the capacity of policymakers to define manageable problems. Some of the topics they suggest should be part of the deconstruction process are helpful in the context of productivity task forces:

- Why does the problem matter, and to whom? The relevance of the problem should be thought in terms of its impact. Is it a problem for only a subset of the high-value fruit producers, or does it affect all of them and even other farmers? Would a solution help unlock growth in a broad sector, or will it only affect a particular group of firms?
- What does it mean to make progress in solving the problem? Is it something that requires two months, a year, or five years? Is everyone who is needed to solve the problem on board with the action plan? Are the different stakeholders aware of the progress being made?
- What are the root causes of the problem? If a task force for the forestry sector decides that the biggest problem is the lack of financial instruments, what are the reasons behind this? Are macroeconomic factors affecting the sector, or have banks not developed instruments that would respond to the industry's specific needs?

Table 2 provides a summary of the key concepts involved in defining productivity constraints along with examples from Namibia.

6.2 How to Identify Policy Solutions?

Once the working group identifies a set of specific problems or constraints, the next step is to find solutions to alleviate or sort them. Much like defining the problems, the discovery and implementation of solutions require "high-bandwidth" policymaking (Hausmann, 2008). The composition of the task force would be diverse enough to act as an information-revealing mechanism, whereby the government and the private sector identify the right problems, brainstorm on their causes and potential solutions, design a plan, and follow through implementation. In the process, each party brings to the table information that is relevant to the mutual interests, but the other party would not have been able to gather on its own. Rather than generating static reports and plans, the focus is on problem-driven solution implementation. The following

Table 2 Defining productivity constraints

Key Concepts	Description	Examples from the Case of High-Value Fruits Productivity Task Force in Namibia
Binding Constraints	These are the most significant issues that hinder productivity in a sector. They guide the task force in prioritizing interventions.	The binding constraints for the industry were market access, access to seeds, and plant health issues. These were the most urgent problems to address for the sector to increase exports.
Profitability Vs. Productivity	Profitability-oriented problems focus on boosting firms' profits but do not necessarily lead to economic growth or investment attraction. Productivity-oriented problems, on the other hand, promote economic growth by enhancing competitiveness.	Instead of directly subsidizing or protecting the sector to increase their short-term profits, the task force worked on solving problems affecting productivity across the board.
Supply- or Demand-Side	Supply-side issues affect firms' productivity through the production process, like the lack of appropriate infrastructure. Demand-side problems, like market access, affect an industry's productivity through scalability.	The task force decided to prioritize a demand-side issue: market access. This decision recognized the importance of scalability in enhancing productivity. A key supply-side issue was accessing essential inputs like seeds. Other supply-side issues, like infrastructure or issues at the border control posts, were also relevant but less urgent for the sector to grow.
	The problems should be decomposed into sub-items, questions, and topics that make them manageable.	The issue of market access was discussed in depth and decomposed into several action areas, out of which the task force decided to focus on China's import protocols in the first place.

Source: Own elaboration

considerations, drawn from the Namibia case, aim to guide this "high-bandwidth" solution-finding process.

6.2.1 Problems versus Goals

There is a trade-off between goals and problems when it comes to defining policy solutions. Policymakers can identify solutions based on their goals or the problems they are trying to fix, and the two methods might result in very different sets of policies. Policymakers often rely heavily on goals for industry-level interventions, and these goals usually include improving indicators or promoting economic growth in the sector. For example, a task force focused on the steel industry can establish import tariffs because the goal is to substitute imports, or they can focus on legal barriers to firm creation because the goal is to improve the "business climate." Although these policies have respectable goals, they might not target the most urgent issues in an industry and, thus, cannot alleviate firms from what is constraining them the most.

Goals give productivity task forces a sense of direction, but they can sometimes become so dominant that they overshadow the specific problems at hand. The danger of being overly goal-oriented is that it can lead to a one-size-fits-all approach, where solutions are shaped more by the goal than by the specific problem they are intended to solve. Problem-oriented solutions, by contrast, are tailored to the unique circumstances and specifics of each problem, requiring a deep understanding of the issues at hand and a willingness to adapt and refine strategies based on the evolving nature of the problems. This approach encourages an iterative process of continuous learning, where the success of a solution is evaluated based on its impact on the problem it was designed to address.

Even if a public–private task force focuses on a nascent industry or a developing technology, problems outweigh or, at least, weigh the same as goals in terms of policy approach. Although the high-value fruits productivity task force in Namibia was focused on an existing industry with a set of problems that needed to be addressed, the NIPDB started a pilot for a task force focused on film and television, a nascent industry that was not developed enough to have a clear assessment of their problems. In our view, this initiative was an example of how a focus on the problems, even for a nascent or new sector, was essential in helping create a business environment in which that sector could thrive.

6.2.2 Feasible versus Pharaonic

Another guiding principle for solution development is that feasibility comes first. Public–private dialogs are often tempted by grandiloquent projects that promise sweeping change. It is natural for discussions to go from generalities to concrete facts, and often focusing on feasible solutions requires deliberate efforts from the participants. While such ambitious projects can be inspiring, they risk creating a gap between the task force's aspirations and what can be accomplished, given resources and limitations. Overly ambitious solutions might also have unintended negative consequences, if the solution disrupts other parts of the system in ways that were not anticipated. In that sense, a solution is feasible when it is mindful of available resources, manageable in the short- to medium-term, and there is a satisfactory level of certainty about its impact.

Solutions must be grounded in a timeline, focusing on what is achievable. This does not imply a rejection of long-term policymaking. Instead, it encourages a pragmatic approach where solutions are executable. Long-term solutions are not necessarily pharaonic. For example, a task force might decide to focus on pursuing a law reform or an infrastructure development, that is, a project that can be complex and ambitious. In that case, it is crucial that the project is decomposed in steps or tasks, that these are assigned to individuals, and that the individuals regularly report on their progress. If the individuals involved in developing the solutions are not made accountable in the working group, they might lack the incentive to make progress.

In the case of Namibia, the possibility of private sector stakeholders identifying problems that were large and expensive to solve was one of the key concerns of government officials in the pre-launching phase. That fear never materialized. The fact that the taskforce identified a few key items or "big tickets" that were definite and actionable – opening Asian markets, joining UPOV convention, facilitating access to imported talent – was one of the key successes of the policy initiative. Others such as access to water and the regime land tenure were less feasible to be addressed in the short term, but still concrete enough to motivate some policy reforms in the short term (tendering Green Schemes to the private sector) and be relevant inputs for medium-term policy planning.

6.2.3 Productivity versus Profitability

As in problem definition, bringing solutions into a productivity task force implies having a focus on productivity over profitability. However, it can be the case that the working group identified a productivity problem but ended up implementing profitability-oriented solutions. One example would be a task force that focuses on the provision of tax incentives for a software development industry. Let us imagine that the initial assessment was that the sector's productivity issue was the shortage of skills: they struggle to find developers that can help them expand their value addition. However, the working group might think that the problem is that the companies do not hire more developers because of profitability issues. Thus, they design a system of tax incentives or rebates for the sector. This might increase the industry's profitability and make it financially feasible to hire more developers and thus, ostensibly increasing productivity. However, this solution does not directly address the core productivity issue. The sector would still have to find the developers. The intervention might overlook this deeper issue by focusing on increasing profitability through tax incentives. While the tax incentives solution is profitability-oriented, it does not necessarily lead to productivity gains or promote overall economic growth. Instead, it could perpetuate an environment where companies rely on external support to maintain profitability rather than improving their internal operations to become more productive and competitive. It also does not guarantee that firms will use the increased profits to hire more personnel and improve productivity. A solution that focused on the productivity issue would aim at skills development by easing restrictions to accessing foreign talent or providing a wage subsidy to the firms over the workers' training period.

In the typology of productive development policies proposed by Crespi et al. (2014), certain policies tend to target profitability rather than productivity issues. They classify policies according to two dimensions: whether they are horizontal or vertical and whether they are public inputs or market interventions. The first dimension refers to the scope of interventions, that is, if they are industry-specific (vertical) or affect the private sector in general (horizontal). The second one refers to the nature of the intervention, that is, if they are public goods that governments provide or interventions in markets that take the form of subsidies, tax breaks, or tariffs, among others. The authors point out that vertical market interventions are the most controversial type of productive development policy. This is because they can lead to rent-seeking behavior in the private sector and favoritism in the public sector (Crespi et al., 2014: 47).

In the case of Namibia, the high-value fruits task force did not end up proposing any market interventions. The lack of essential public inputs was noteworthy, so any potential rent-seeking behavior in the private sector was overshadowed by the need for government support in terms of plant health and market access. This situation accentuated the vital role that the public sector can play in the development of new industries. A role that consisted not in transferring direct subsidies, but in providing the essential resources needed to enable competitiveness in both domestic and international markets.

6.2.4 Experimental Approach

Finally, the adoption of an experimental approach is of great help to find and implement solutions. The critical idea is that prioritizing master plans, policy reports, or research-heavy engagements makes the public–private collaboration slow, expensive, and risk-averse. If the public sector officials must wait until having a comprehensive analytical view of the problems, then the policy process would necessarily slow down to a point of inertia. In turn, extensive reports and master plans tend to be too expensive for the knowledge needed to do industrial policy at the sector level. Additionally, research-oriented working groups tend to stay close to evidence when it comes to making decisions about policy interventions. This might result in high levels of risk aversion, given that knowledge and resources are limited. While research reports can provide comprehensive information about a problem, they do not necessarily yield actionable solutions. Moreover, they may not be responsive enough to productivity task forces' fast-paced and dynamic nature.

Although technical capacity is critical, it should not dominate the decision-making process. As discussed in Section 3, the high-value fruits productivity task force significantly benefited from research contributions and policy memos. These resources allowed participants to comprehend the potential scale within the sector and supplied comparative analysis through the lens of international cases. Moreover, these inputs spurred valuable analyses that contributed to a deeper understanding of the productivity problems and suggested possible policy interventions.

An experimental approach encourages a culture of learning by doing. It involves testing ideas, gathering feedback, analyzing results, and iterating on solutions. This process is more agile and responsive to changes in the industry environment. The solution discovery and implementation processes are not always straightforward and require a learning-by-doing approach. The iterative nature of the solution-finding process is crucial for avoiding impractical interventions, building mechanisms of trust amongst the stakeholders, and developing resistance to failure. The working group needs to be able to go back to its definitions and question them, adapt to a changing environment, and be flexible enough to coordinate multiple agendas. This ensures that solutions are effective and align with the task force's overarching objectives. It also allows for a more robust and nuanced understanding of the problems, as solutions are tested and adjusted in real-world contexts rather than being developed in the abstract.

Table 3 provides a summary of the key concepts involved in defining solutions for productivity constraints along with examples from Namibia.

Table 3 Defining solutions

Key Concept	Description	Example from the Case of High-Value Fruits Productivity Task Force in Namibia
Problems vs. Goals	The balance between defining policy solutions based on goals or problems. Goals give direction but can overshadow specific problems, whereas problem-oriented solutions require a deep understanding of each unique problem.	The task force focused on an existing industry with a set of problems that needed to be addressed. They also piloted a task force focused on the film and television industry, a nascent field without a clear assessment of its problems.
Feasible vs. Pharaonic	Solution development should prioritize feasibility over grandiose change. Given resources and limitations, ambitious projects can create a gap between aspirations and feasibility.	In Namibia, the task force identified water and land tenure access as constraints for high-value fruits sector development. However, these were less feasible to address in the medium term, so they decided to focus on other issues.
Productivity vs. Profitability	Task forces should focus on productivity rather than profitability. Solutions should target core productivity issues, not profitability ones, which could perpetuate an environment of external reliance rather than internal improvements.	Namibia's high-value fruits task force did not propose any vertical market interventions, which typically target profitability. They recognized the need for government support in terms of plant health and market access.
Experimental Approach	Adopting an experimental approach can be beneficial for solution finding and implementation. This involves testing ideas, analyzing results, and iterating on solutions, making the working group more agile and responsive.	Research was not the leading voice in setting and implementing the working group's agenda. In turn, the participants collaborated in developing solutions and learning during the process. The group had an experimental approach to productive policy development.

Source: Own elaboration

7 Conclusions

The end of the super commodity price cycle left Namibia with significant twin deficits in its fiscal and current accounts and a legacy of high and increasing foreign debt. Social and welfare gains achieved during the growth acceleration registered between 2000 and 2015 had started to erode. In 2018, President Hage Geingob was reelected with the lowest share of the votes in the short history of the country (54%), threatening the dominant position of the political party South-West Africa People's Organization (SWAPO) for the first time in twenty-eight years.

In that context, the government started to look for and develop different ways to partner with the private sector and attract foreign direct investment into sectors with export potential. A group of more private-sector friendly government officials – many from the private sector – were appointed to key positions in Cabinet and the President's office. The Namibian Investment Promotion and Development Board (NIPDB) was created in 2019 under Section 21 of the Companies Act and put at the level of the Office of the President. That feature allowed the board to hire the talent required and act without the restrictions that regulations typically impose on formal public sector entities. The Harvard Growth Lab started a research project to support the government in searching for sectors with the potential to attract investment and deliver export-led growth and identify the most binding constraints preventing that potential from realizing. That research effort yielded various inputs which gradually found their way into policy initiatives in different areas such as macroeconomic strategy, sovereign wealth and stabilization fund (the Welwitschia Fund), renewable energy policy, and various initiatives to improve the relationship with private sector stakeholders at home and abroad led by the NIPDB. That was the context in which PTFs were conceived and launched.

This case study summarized Namibia's experience with the high-value fruit productivity task force. To the extent of our knowledge, this is the first documented experience with PPDs at the sector level in Africa that follows the methodology initially established by Piero Ghezzi in Peru's Mesas Ejecutivas. Public–private dialogs are a smart and efficient way for the government to gain a deep understanding of business dynamics at the sector level. They work as information-revelation mechanisms that enable both parties to gather intelligence about each other and work together to alleviate or sort out the most relevant constraints identified. We hope to offer insights into the transformative power of public–private collaboration in promoting economic growth, contribute to the growing literature on the topic, and provide a practical roadmap for policy practitioners to launch similar initiatives in different contexts. We have summarized our learnings across three key policy insights.

The first critical insight is the importance of political authorization and the participation of high-level government officials in the task force. The high-value fruit task force was chaired by the Minister of Finance and attended by the Director General of the Minister of Agriculture, Water and Land Reform, and the Director for Investment of the Namibian Investment Promotion and Development Board. In a country without a strong tradition of PPD, that presence signaled the endeavor's importance to private sector stakeholders and created significant momentum. The importance of this cannot be underscored. Coordination was needed across different government agencies to sort the constraints identified by the task force. Government officials from the most relevant (to the sector) entities conveyed a strong sense of possibility to which the farmers reacted positively and constructively. Conversely, the withdrawal of these key actors in the third year and their replacement with government officials of lower rank was perceived as a loss of interest, and from then onwards, the meetings went on at a lower frequency.

The second insight is that choosing the right sector to start with is a stepping stone. Although the high-value fruits PTF had several downsides and was not a success in terms of policy change, working with a proper first sector allowed the government team to learn from the experience, adapt the framework to the local context, and get the necessary political authorization to expand the initiative to other sectors. As in the case of the forestry sector in Peru's Mesas Ejecutivas, the high-value fruits sector in Namibia had evident growth potential. Additionally, grape, dates and berries' farmers showed from the outset a strong willingness to collaborate with the public sector. The sector also lacked political visibility, which gave the team the necessary space to experiment and adapt to the Namibian context. By focusing on one sector with significant potential as a pilot, there is a higher possibility of success, which would create momentum among other sectors to demand the launching of additional task forces. Internally, starting with the right sector can help the coordinating team gain confidence and build the capacity they need in a context that is not overly complicated nor too challenging for a first experience.

The third insight is that PTF needs to target the correct issues during the meetings. In the case of Namibia, one of the fears of government officials was that private sector stakeholders would demand actions that would imply significant public investments the government did not have the means to finance. On the private sector side, the fear was that the discussion would drift to broader political and economic issues that would not lead to concrete action or significant improvement. The emphasis on productivity and actionable items, coupled with the flexibility to adapt to different topics emerging from discussions, was instrumental in achieving progress. That helped the NIPDB develop relevant information that guided the discussions and led to identifying relatively small, concrete, and feasible actions to remove significant constraints. Achieving that in the early meetings was one of the most significant successes of the task force in Namibia.

At the time of writing, the high-value fruit task force has been meeting for nearly three years. According to all participants, the most significant breakthrough has been to expedite the processing of work permits to attract foreign talent and consultants to Namibia. That was achieved relatively early in the process. On the other big tickets – UPOV convention, access to the Chinese market, access to water, and land tenure – issues have been thoroughly discussed and well diagnosed, but no definite progress has been made. However, the task force continues to meet. Ideally, these should be temporary public–private working groups that should stop once all the relevant constraints have been addressed or once the government capacity to sort out the issues has been exhausted. The latter seems to describe the status of the high-value fruit task force. High-level government officials withdrew from the task force two years into the initiative, and grape farmers did the same around the same time. A smaller group of dates and blueberry farmers continues to meet with public officials of lower rank. Why?

In a country that raised from a legacy of apartheid and where significant distrust has prevailed between private sector stakeholders and government officials, PTFs seem to be providing a space where these parties meet with some agenda to discuss issues of mutual interest. Participants consider that as a channel to remain in touch and has value in itself – regardless of whether progress on relevant issues is made or not. In countries where other instances exist, such as chambers of commerce, private sector guilds, and government forums, these meetings would have lost convening capacity much earlier.

By the end of 2023, two years after the launch of the PTF, some of the fastest-growing companies in Namibia came from the high-value fruits sector. The PTFs undeniably helped to create and nurture a better business environment. The discussions have informed government policy more broadly and led to policy initiatives aimed at gradually improving the incentives for private sector stakeholders to increase their participation in agriculture. The sector's economic performance is positive. We know that correlation does not imply causation and that these developments might have occurred in a counterfactual scenario where productivity task forces did not occur. However, the task forces did started a process of PPDs with positive takeaways for both sides.

References

African Banker Awards (2024). https://africanbankerawards.com/.

Amukeshe, L. (2023, May 20). Namibia's fastest-growing companies 2023. *The Namibian*. www.namibian.com.na/namibias-fastest-growing-companies-2023/.

Andrews, M. (2013). *The Limits of Institutional Reform in Development: Changing Rules for Realistic Solutions (1st ed.)*. Cambridge University Press. https://doi.org/10.1017/CBO9781139060974.

Andrews, M., Pritchett, L., & Woolcock, M. (2017). *Building State Capability: Evidence, Analysis, Action (1st ed.)*. Oxford University Press.

Baer, W. (1972). Import substitution and industrialization in Latin America: Experiences and interpretations. *Latin American Research Review*, 7(1), 95–122.

Crespi, G., Fernández-Arias, E., & Stein, E. (Eds.). (2014). *Rethinking Productive Development*. Palgrave Macmillan. https://doi.org/10.1057/9781137393999.

Dell, J. (2023, February 26). Fishrot: The corruption scandal entwining Namibia and Iceland, *BBC*, www.bbc.com/news/world-africa-64526018.

Devlin, R., & Pietrobelli, C. (2016). *Modern Industrial Policy and Public–Private Councils at the Subnational Level: Empirical Evidence from Mexico*. Inter-American Development Bank.

Fabricius, P. (2022, February 18). Namibia's Fishrot trial will test the scales of justice, *ISS Today*, Institute for Security Studies, https://issafrica.org/iss-today/namibias-fishrot-trial-will-test-the-scales-of-justice.

FAO (2023a). Table of Adopted Standards (ISPMs). www.ippc.int/en/core-activities/standards-setting/ispms/.

FAO (2023b). *Fishery and Aquaculture Country Profiles: Namibia*. www.fao.org/fishery/en/facp/nam?lang=en.

Fernandez-Arias, E., Sabel, C., Stein, E., & Trejos, A. (2016). *Two to Tango: Public-Private Collaboration for Productive Development Policies*. Inter-American Development Bank.

Financial Times & Statista (2023). *Africa's Fastest Growing Companies 2023*. https://r.statista.com/en/growth-champions/africas-fastest-growing-companies-2023/ranking/.

Food Business Africa (2023, September 2). Namibia Berries to invest US$80M over 7 years to boost blueberries production. www.foodbusinessafrica.com/

namibia-berries-to-invest-us80m-over-7-years-to-boost-blueberries-production/.

Fortunato, A., & Enciso, S. (2023). *Food for Growth: A Diagnostics of Namibia's Agriculture Sector*. CID Research Fellow and Graduate Student Working Paper No. 154. Center for International Development at Harvard University. www.tinyurl.com/yswb6b9q.

Fresh Plaza (2024). Walvis Bay is Namibian grape growers' answer to Cape Town Port. February 29. www.freshplaza.com/north-america/article/9581735/walvis-bay-is-namibian-grape-growers-answer-to-cape-town-port/.

Ghezzi, P. (2017). Mesas Ejecutivas in Peru: Lessons for Productive development policies. *Global Policy*, *8*(3), 369–380. https://doi.org/10.1111/1758-5899.12457.

Ghezzi, P. (2019). *Mesas ejecutivas en Perú: Una tecnología para el desarrollo productivo*. Inter-American Development Bank. https://doi.org/10.18235/0001856.

Gómez Restrepo, H., & Mitchell, D. (2016). *Comisiones regionales de competitividad de Colombia: Lecciones para su fortalecimiento Institucional*. IDB-TN-959. Inter-American Development Bank.

González, A. L., Hallak, J. C., Scattolo, G., & Tacsir, A. (2022). The need for coordination to develop customized competitiveness in agrifood systems: Lemon, pork, and dairy in Argentina. *Journal of Agribusiness in Developing and Emerging Economies*, *12*(4), 750–767. https://doi.org/10.1108/JADEE-10-2021-0271.

Hallak, J. C., & López, A. (2022). *¿Cómo apoyar la internacionalización productiva en América Latina?: Análisis de políticas, requerimientos de capacidades estatales y riesgos*. Banco Interamericano de Desarrollo. https://doi.org/10.18235/0004650.

Hausmann, R. (2008). The other hand: High bandwidth development policy. *SSRN Electronic Journal*. HKS Working Paper No. RWP08-060, Available at SSRN: https://doi.org/10.2139/ssrn.1314799.

Hausmann, R., Klinger, B., & Wagner, R. (2008). *Doing Growth Diagnostics in Practice: A "Mindbook"*, CID Working Papers 177, Center for International Development at Harvard University.

Hausmann, R., Santos, M. A., Barrios, D. et al. (2022). *A Growth Diagnostic of Namibia*, CID Faculty Working Paper No. 405. February. Center for International Development at Harvard University. https://growthlab.cid.harvard.edu/publications/growth-diagnostic-namibia.

Henley, J. (2019, November 15). Bribery allegations over fishing rights rock Iceland and Namibia. *The Guardian*, www.theguardian.com/world/2019/nov/15/bribery-allegations-over-fishing-rights-rock-iceland-and-namibia.

Hidalgo, C. A., & Hausmann, R. (2009). The building blocks of economic complexity. *Proceedings of the National Academy of Sciences*, *106*(26), 10570–10575. https://doi.org/10.1073/pnas.0900943106.

InvestSA (2020). *Investing in South Africa's Cosmetics and Personal Care Sector*, Department of Trade and Industry, Republic of South Africa. www.investsa.gov.za/wp-content/uploads/2021/03/FACT-SHEET_COSMETICS_2020.pdf.

IPPR & Transparency International Iceland (2022). FISHROT three years on: A call for restorative justice, https://ippr.org.na/publication/fishrot-a-call-for-restorative-justice/.

Jaurequiberry, F., & Tappata, M. (2022). The role of public-private coordination: The case of sweet cherries in Argentina 2000–2020. Documentos de Trabajo 2022/04. Universidad Torcuato Di Tella, Escuela de Gobierno. www.utdt.edu/ver_contenido.php?id_contenido=22871&id_item_menu=31549.

Juhász, R., Lane, N., Oehlsen, E., & Pérez, V. C. (2022). *The Who, What, When, and How of Industrial Policy: A Text-Based Approach* [Preprint]. SocArXiv. https://doi.org/10.31235/osf.io/uyxh9.

Kimani, E. (2018, November 21). Benefits of Plant Variety Protection and UPOV Membership: The Case of Kenya. *European Seed*. https://european-seed.com/2018/11/benefits-of-plant-variety-protection-and-upov-membership-the-case-of-kenya/.

Koike, O. (1994). Bureaucratic policy-making in Japan: Role and function of deliberation Councils. In Jun, J. S. (Ed.). *Development in the Asia Pacific: A Public Policy Perspective*. W. de Gruyter, 433–448.

Lane, N. (2020). The new empirics of industrial policy. *Journal of Industry, Competition and Trade*, *20*(2), 209–234. https://doi.org/10.1007/s10842-019-00323-2.

Lewis, Colin M. (2019). Revisiting industrial policy and industrialization in twentieth century Latin America. *Journal of Latin American Studies*, *51*(4), 725–745.

L'Oréal (2023). *Universal Registration Document*. www.loreal-finance.com/system/files/2024-03/LOREAL_2023_Universal_Registration_Document_en.pdf.

McMillan, M., Rodrik, D., & Verduzco-Gallo, Í. (2014). Globalization, structural change, and productivity growth, with an update on Africa. *World Development*, *63*, 11–32. https://doi.org/10.1016/j.worlddev.2013.10.012.

Meintjes, F. (2023, December 5). Walvis Bay in Namibia plays key role in early Southern African grape exports. *Fuitnet*. www.fruitnet.com/eurofruit/walvis-bay-in-namibia-plays-key-role-in-early-southern-african-grape-exports/257430.article.

Meintjes, F. (2024, January 15). Cape Town port issues escalate. *Fruitnet*. www.fruitnet.com/main-navigation/cape-town-port-issues-escalate/257948.article.

Melber, H. (2005). Land & politics in Namibia. *Review of African Political Economy, 32*(103), 135–142. Imperialism & African Social Formations (March), www.jstor.org/stable/4006914.

Melber, H. (2014). *Understanding Namibia: The Trials of Independence*. Oxford University Press.

Namibian Agronomic Board (2023). *An Overview of the Status Quo of Fruit Production in Namibia*. www.nab.com.na/wp-content/uploads/2023/03/Research-article-AN-OVERVIEW-OF-THE-STATUS-QOU-OF-FRUITS-PRODUCTION-IN-NAMIBIA.pdf.

Obaya, M., & Stein, E. H. (2021). El diálogo público-privado para la formulación de políticas productivas: La experiencia de las mesas sectoriales en Argentina (2016–2019). Inter-American Development Bank. https://doi.org/10.18235/0003132.

Republic of Namibia (1995). Agricultural Land Reform Act, Government Gazette of the Republic of Namibia No. 1040, 3 March 1995, pp. 1–65. https://www.fao.org/faolex/results/details/en/c/LEX-FAOC004463/#:~:text=An%20Act%20to%20provide%20for,have%20been%20socially%2C%20economically%20or.

Rodrik, D. (2004). *Industrial Policy for the Twenty-First Century*. http://tinyurl.com/y9yjzpdq.

Rodrik, D. (2015). *Premature Deindustrialization*. Working Paper No. 20935. National Bureau of Economic Research. https://doi.org/10.3386/w20935.

Ruiton Cabanillas, J., Hidalgo Romero, I., & Figueroa Sánchez, A. E. (2022). La inversión pública en riego y el crecimiento económico del sector agrario en el Perú en el período 2001-2015. *Gobierno Y Gestión Pública, 5*(1). https://portalrevistas.aulavirtualusmp.pe/index.php/RevistaGobiernoyG/article/view/2337.

Sabel, C., & Jordan, L. (2015). Doing, Learning, Being: Some Lessons Learned from Malaysia's National Transformation Program, Competitive Industries and Innovation Program (CIIP) and World Bank Group. https://documentos.bancomundial.org/es/publication/documents-reports/documentdetail/464231565116506887/doing-learning-being-some-lessons-learned-from-malaysias-national-transformation-program.

Schneider, B. R. (2015). *Designing Industrial Policy in Latin America*. Palgrave Macmillan. https://doi.org/10.1057/9781137524843.

Statista (2024). *Market Insights Fish & Seafood*. www.statista.com/outlook/cmo/food/fish-seafood/worldwide.

References

US Embassy Windhoek (2022). *Namibian Marula Oil makes it to America*, https://na.usembassy.gov/namibian-marula-oil-makes-it-to-america/.

USA International Trade Administration, ITA (2024). Namibia: Commercial Fishing Country Guide, www.trade.gov/country-commercial-guides/namibia-commercial-fishing.

World Bank (2011). *Public-Private Dialogue for Sector Competitiveness and Local Economic Development: Lessons from the Mediterranean Region.* www.publicprivatedialogue.org/papers/Public%20Private%20Dialogue%20for%20Sector%20Competitiveness%20and%20Local%20Economic%20Development.pdf.

World Bank (2017). *Gaining Momentum in Peruvian Agriculture: Opportunities to Increase Productivity and Enhance Competitiveness*, Agriculture Global Practice, World Bank Group. https://documents1.worldbank.org/curated/en/107451498513689693/pdf/P162084-06-26-2017-1498513685623.pdf.

World Bank (2024). *The Container Port Performance Index 2023: A Comparable Assessment of Performance Based on Vessel Time in Port*. CPPI. © World Bank. http://hdl.handle.net/10986/39824.

Abbreviations

ARIPO	– African Regional Intellectual Property Organization
BoN	– Bank of Namibia
ECI	– Economic Complexity Index
ME	– Mesa Ejecutiva
MTI	– Ministry of Trade and Industrialization of Namibia
MOF	– Ministry of Finance of Namibia
MAWLR	– Ministry of Agriculture, Water, and Land Reform of Namibia
NIPDB	– Namibian Investment and Development Board
NTF	– Namibia Trade Forum
PPD	– Public-private dialog
PTF	– Productivity task force
SWAPO	– South-West Africa People's Organization
SENASA	– Servicio Nacional de Sanidad Agraria del Perú
UPOV	– International Union for the Protection of New Varieties of Plants

Acknowledgments

This case study is a by-product of an applied research project conducted by the Harvard Growth Lab in Namibia from 2020 to 2023, with support from the Bank of Namibia.[1] The project's goal was to identify economic sectors with the potential to deliver export-led growth and employment, categorize the most binding constraints preventing that potential from realizing, and support the government in the design and implementation of data-driven policy recommendations to improve Namibia's competitiveness. Within that context, the Growth Lab team presented the government officials with the idea of productivity task forces, which was quickly incorporated into the policy process and brought to implementation.

We want to express our sincere thanks to Johannes Gawaxab (President of the Bank of Namibia), Ebson Uanguta (Deputy Governor of the Bank of Namibia), Ipumbu Shiimi (Minister of Finance and Public Enterprises), Obeth Kandjoze (Director General of the National Planning Commission), Nangula Nelulu Uaandja (CEO of the Namibia Investment Promotion and Development Board, NIPDB), Penda Ithindi (Director General at Ministry of Agriculture, Water, and Land Reform), Helvi Fillipus (Deputy Director at Ministry of Finance and Public Enterprises), François van Schalkwyk (Executive Director of Investment and Sector Development at NIPDB), Tinus Fourie (Manager of Research and Development at NIPDB), and Bernie Zaaruka (Macroeconomics and Public Finance Specialist).

We are also grateful to the Harvard Growth Lab team in Namibia. Under the intellectual leadership of Ricardo Hausmann, we gathered an amazing group of people from different backgrounds and skill sets, which contributed to the overall success of the three-year engagement: Douglas Barrios, Nikita Taniparti, Jorge Tudela, Fernando García, Jorge Tapia, Sheyla Enciso-Valdivia, Alexia Lochman, and Sophia Henn.

We were lucky to have as reviewers of this Element two of the scholars and policy practitioners that have contributed the most to the literature on public-private dialogs at the sector level. Bailey Klinger integrated the Harvard Growth Lab team as an external consultant to bring his experience in the Peruvian *Mesas Ejecutivas* into the design and implementation of productivity taskforces in Namibia. The paper also benefited from the generous and

---

[1] More information about the project is available here: https://growthlab.hks.harvard.edu/policy-research/namibia.

abundant feedback from Ernesto Stein, who provided insights and suggestions from more than thirty years of experience working in productive development policies in Latin America and with public-private dialogs at the sector level in Argentina. The usual disclaimers apply.

Cambridge Elements

Economics of Emerging Markets

Bruno S. Sergi
Harvard University

Editor Bruno S. Sergi is an Instructor at Harvard University, an Associate of the Harvard University Davis Center for Russian and Eurasian Studies and Harvard University Asia Center. He is the Academic Series Editor of the Cambridge *Elements in the Economics of Emerging Markets* (Cambridge University Press), a co-editor of the *Lab for Entrepreneurship and Development* book series, and associate editor of *The American Economist*. Concurrently, he teaches International Political Economics at the University of Messina, Scientific Director of the Lab for Entrepreneurship and Development (LEAD), and a co-founder and Scientific Director of the International Center for Emerging Markets Research at RUDN University in Moscow. He has published over 200 articles in professional journals and twenty-one books as author, co-author, editor, and co-editor.

About the Series

The aim of this Elements series is to deliver state-of-the-art, comprehensive coverage of the knowledge developed to date, including the dynamics and prospects of these economies, focusing on emerging markets' economics, finance, banking, technology advances, trade, demographic challenges, and their economic relations with the rest of the world, as well as the causal factors and limits of economic policy in these markets.

Cambridge Elements

Economics of Emerging Markets

Elements in the Series

Banking Sector Reforms: Is China Following Japan's Footstep?
M. Kabir Hassan and Mohammad Dulal Miah

COVID-19 and Islamic Finance
M. Kabir Hassan and Aishath Muneeza

Harnessing Sovereign Wealth Funds in Emerging Economies toward Sustainable Development
Mona Mostafa El-Sholkamy and Mohammad Habibur Rahman

The Emerging Economies under the Dome of the Fourth Industrial Revolution
Mark Esposito and Amit Kapoor

On the Road to Economic Prosperity: The Role of Infrastructure in Ghana
Tuan Anh Luong and Zenas Azuma

Banking Stability and Financial Conglomerates in European Emerging Countries
Pavla Klepková Vodová, Iveta Palečková and Daniel Stavárek

The Paradox of Gender Equality and Economic Outcomes in Sub-Saharan Africa: The Role of Land Rights
Evelyn F. Wamboye

Mobile Banking and Access to Public Services in Bangladesh: Influencing Issues and Factors
M. Kabir Hassan, Jannatul Ferdous and Hasanul Banna

BRICS and the Global Financial Order: Liberalism Contested?
Johannes Petry and Andreas Nölke

Global South Leadership Style: Strategies for Navigating Emerging Market
Abel Femi Adekola, Mona Pearl, Bruno S. Sergi and Richard J. Muszynski III

Digitalization in Emerging Economies
Mark Esposito, Yusaf Akbar and Francis Xavier Campbell

Public–Private Dialogs to Spur Export-led Growth: The Case of Productivity Taskforces in Namibia
Andrés Fortunato and Miguel Angel Santos

A full series listing is available at: www.cambridge.org/EEM

For EU product safety concerns, contact us at Calle de José Abascal, 56–1°,
28003 Madrid, Spain or eugpsr@cambridge.org.

www.ingramcontent.com/pod-product-compliance
Ingram Content Group UK Ltd.
Pitfield, Milton Keynes, MK11 3LW, UK
UKHW021509110325
456069UK00006B/514